FINDING GOD'S
SECRET PLACE

FINDING GOD'S
SECRET PLACE

Walking in the Power and Light of the Almighty God

DR. AKEAM AMONIPHIS SIMMONS

FINDING GOD'S SECRET PLACE
WALKING IN THE POWER AND LIGHT OF THE ALMIGHTY GOD

ALL SCRIPTURE VERSES USED IN THIS BOOK IS TAKEN FROM THE KING JAMES VERSION OF THE BIBLE

iUniverse books may be ordered through booksellers or by contacting:

iUniverse
1663 Liberty Drive
Bloomington, IN 47403
www.iuniverse.com
1-800-Authors (1-800-288-4677)

Because of the dynamic nature of the Internet, any web addresses or links contained in this book may have changed since publication and may no longer be valid. The views expressed in this work are solely those of the author and do not necessarily reflect the views of the publisher, and the publisher hereby disclaims any responsibility for them.

Any people depicted in stock imagery provided by Thinkstock are models, and such images are being used for illustrative purposes only. Certain stock imagery © Thinkstock.

ISBN: 978-1-5320-3197-7 (sc)
ISBN: 978-1-5320-3198-4 (e)

Print information available on the last page.

iUniverse rev. date: 09/01/2017

HE THAT DWELL IN THE SECRET PLACE OF THE MOST HIGH SHALL ABIDE UNDER THE SHADOW OF THE ALMIGHTY.

I WILL SAY OF THE LORD, HE IS MY REFUGE AND MY FORTRESS; MY GOD; IN HIM WILL I TRUST.

SURELY HE SHALL DELIVER YOU FROM THE SNARE OF THE FOWLER, AND FROM THE NOISOME PESTILENCE.

PSALM 91: 1-3

TO SUCCEED AND ACHIEVE YOUR DESTINY

YOU MUST BELIEVE IN A POWER
THAT IS GREATER THAN YOU

A SUPERNATURAL POWER OUTSIDE OF YOURSELF

GOD JEHOVAH IS THE ALMIGHTY POWER!!!!!!

To my daughters

Nequisa and Keandra

Who forced me to stay focused

To my grandchildren

Markayla M. Simmons

Who has faithfully believed in me as a writer

Kimyrin

Who always wants to be in charge no matter what

Aiden

Who is slowly coming into his own

To my wife

Who saw the King in me and spoke it into reality

CONTENTS

FOREWORD

While perusing the condition of our beloved country, the melting pot of the world, it became quite apparent to me that we are collectively wrestling with some very deep, sometimes generational, problems. Problems that are not so easily solved or even seen without trained eyes.

And, perhaps it is so very easy for those outside looking in to overly simplify our struggles, and prescribe us a readily made all fixing cure-a cure that has failed innumerable times before amongst the masses.

Like sheep, they have ushered us in hoping to shear away our hurt, pain, and our struggles; only to find that it is far too deeply rooted to wipe away with just a whim.

And even though, most of the struggles for which we go through, we have put ourselves in, or had a lot to do with, still we need a "Savior" that will afford us the comfort and security of His protective light in His secret place. There, we can go to Him unashamedly with all of our burdens, and all of our struggles, and all of our weaknesses, and all of our shortcomings, and all of our failures, and rest at His feet without too harsh judgment-just comforted by His grace and His mercy that is always accompanied by His divine peace.

Yes, we need a power that is outside of us that can invade us and keep us during our pervasive times of struggle, need, pain, and despair. A power that is bigger than what we are going through-something that is greater than us!

We need something that is greater than us to get us through when we are going through, or when we feel like giving up and declaring that we are just done and through-when we become sick and tired of being sick and tired.

I have been pastoring for more than thirty-five years, in four different churches. What I have discovered is the thread that connects and runs through all of them, the norm amidst all of them is that "everybody" is struggling and going through something; every family and most individuals are dealing with a great degree of a painful situation, or condition, or circumstance of some sort-from finances, sickness, to emotional duress, we're all suffering and dealing with some very private debilitating issues that causes us no end of shame, discomfort, pain, and hurt.

Hurt pervades the congregation, and if it pervades the congregation, then, it is safe to conclude that hurt, emotional hurt, bombards our streets and homes, for out of the home and off the streets comes the church. Our pews are filled with hurting people because our streets and homes are filled with hurting people.

Amidst all of the cataclysm surrounding us, and in the world at large, we find ourselves attempting to wrestle with some things for which we have not been fully prepared to deal with.

Nobody taught us how to break the curses that are filled with pain and have been plaguing our families throughout each generation- an intensity of pain and hurt that none can adequately describe. So, we roam from pillow to post trying to hide, or at the very least, circumvent our hurt that is more than mere discomfort or discontent.

Hence, we flock to the church of brick and mortar hoping to find a remedy for our hurt and emotional ailments; only to find a pulpit usually graced by a man who is bent on making us feel good, so that we can give a bigger offering. Nine out of ten of the pulpits are bellowing about how the congregants can get more wealth, have more, and break through into financial blessings; what they fail to realize is that "having more" does not heal our emotional, psychological, and turmoil filled life. Sometimes, having more stuff increases our problems. Most are dealing with some deep darkened issues; issues that require some "in touch" sessions with God.

A few days ago I spoke confidentially to a young man that was struggling with homosexuality. He said to me, "I am trying Reverend, but it is so hard, and people are so judgmental in the church. There are times that I go to church, and have to leave because the preacher or speaker is gay bashing."

I prayed with him and told him to follow God, and not listen to the people that perhaps hadn't gotten in God to where they should be-to be able to love and look beyond one's faults and see their need, and love them in-spite of their sins.

The young man or young woman that is struggling with homosexuality or homosexual tendencies comes to the church for help and guidance, only to sometimes find a place that is filled with a great degree of stone throwers looking for someone to throw at; even the preacher, for the struggling young man, who is already convicted by his own conscious, hears bellowing and echoing from the pulpit sentences like, "God made Adam and Eve, not Adam and Steve." The congregation burst out in a loud cheer of Amen; so the young man or woman who is struggling with the dis-ease silently keep their demon to themselves for fear of being ridiculed and demonized by the congregants and the insensitive pastor that is trying to make the people feel good at the expense of a struggling few. Just ridiculing is not going to bring about deliverance and help them break free.

Or, how about the brother or sister, who is faithful in the church, now has to walk through the church doors with the unpleasant stigma of a painful divorce (I've been there). They are embarrassed and ashamed and desperately need to find God's secret place and His light to shield them from the callous people's (that sometimes mean well) judgment. Somebody has to minister to them and tell them that there is still life after a horrific divorce, and that God forgives divorcees too.

When the clergy fails us, we journey to the other man that can make us feel good and cover up our hurt and emotional distraught-the pharmacist.

350 million people in the world suffer with depression-5% of the world's population; 30 million of those are in the United States of

America, and most are females. Depression is the leading cause of disability.

8% of our youth between the ages of 18-22 suffer from some degree of depression.

Americans spend millions and millions of dollars annually on antidepressants drugs alone.

Thus, people are hurting everywhere, and depression is just the peak of the iceberg.

Many carry their hurt around in their bosom privately because most don't know how to deal with the hurting problem.

Some of the hurt and pain that many are confronted with are:

1. Failed marriages
2. Broken homes
3. Homosexuality
4. Breaking the grips of homosexuality
5. Broken relationships
6. Desertion
7. Hopelessness
8. Loveless
9. Unfaithfulness
10. Homelessness

The list is endless; it goes on and on, etc.....etc.....etc.

Because of all of the hurt, there is an urgent need for the supernatural power of Jehovah God to prevail in our lives. His secret place will hide us and help us to deal with the problems that cause the hurt in our lives. But, finding God seems to be illusive and very convoluted. Still, it does not deter us from the thirst to find His secret place and walk in His light of salvation.

HOW DO WE FIND HIM-GOD'S SECRET PLACE!!!!

Every generation, from the very beginning of mankind, has always had a deep burning and unyielding quest to find and know God-its creator; but very few men have come to truly know and understand their creator. They search the world over through religions, churches, monasteries, books, songs, hymns, stories, and travels, trying to find God; so the prevailing question becomes, then, **where is God?**

This search for God should seem illogical seeing that, just in the United States alone, there are over 450,000 churches, and over 200 different denominations that proclaim the existence of God, and that they know Him; so thus, it would appear that the answer to the pervading question of where is God, would seem to be, go to the churches, and there you will find God, but no, not so simple. The local church has become inundated with superficial programs and conferences and the like, trying to cover up the fact that God has become a surreptitious part of them.

Most of the proclaimed churches have less than a hundred members, with all of them directing a different path to finding God. But, a closer observation declares and decry that many walk in the midst of confusion-just walking blindly in the footsteps of others who are engulfed in a mass of simplistic confusion-the blind leading the blind.

Amongst all of the various churches professing themselves to be a guild to God, we also have over a million Muslims in the United States declaring their knowledge of God, Allah as they so passionately calls Him. But still, no one has conveyed God; not even through their "so called" Godly principles-principles of which they themselves seldom fully adhere to, so the question still remains, **where is God?**

This book is an attempt to reveal the **secret place** where God resides; for not everyone will find Him. It becomes a "secret place" because, though many seek Him, few have found Him.

Many have searched the world, searching for the great God of the universe, but none have yet to declare, "Here, here, here is God; come see Him for yourself." No, they build pretty buildings, and tell us that God is in the building, but I don't see him. They tell us that God is in the text that we read, but I don't see Him; they tell us that He is in the very air that we breathe, but still, I don't feel or see Him; so, **where is God?..........**Let's see......

CHAPTER ONE

FROM THE BEGINNING

The first recording of God is in the bible, in the book of Genesis. Note the first mentioning of Him: Genesis 1:1: In the beginning God created the heaven and the earth.

There is not given a record of His beginning, or where He came from. God just appears in the records of men. So thus, it does appear that "God is" and always has been-according to the record. He has no beginning and has no ending. God is not similar to anything that we know, for all things have a beginning and an ending, but not the supreme God.

Jesus, who says that He and God are one, says this of the matter in Revelation 1:8:

I am Alpha and Omega, the beginning and the ending, says the Lord, which is, and which was, and which is to come, the Almighty.

Jesus stresses again, at the close of the book of Revelation, that God is Alpha and Omega – Revelation 22:13.

Jesus asserts that God, Jehovah, is and always has been, but though, He has always been and always is, it is still, none-the less, most difficult to find Him.

Note what the bible says in Genesis 1: 26-27:

26. And God said. "Let us make man in our image, after our likeness: and let them have dominion over the fish of the sea, and over the fowl of the air, and over the cattle, and over all the earth, and over every creeping thing that creeps upon the earth.
27. So God created man in hi own image, in the image of God created hi him: male and female created he them.

So thus, we were made in God's image and after His likeness; which means that we-mankind, was made to be just like God, our creator; the creature immolates its creator.

Because of the way that we were made, in each of us, there is a distinct yearning for relationship with our creator. There is an unconscious passion buried deep within us to be "like" God. We are driven to seek our God because "the power" of our God rests deep within us. It defines who we are. "The power" is what differs man from every other creature that God made. Man is the only one that inhabits the power of the creator; he is the only creature that God made that is able to exhibit and facilitate the power habits of God. It drives him to conquer and thirst for superiority; for he is superior to everything that God made.

Many men cannot explain this drive, so they try to fulfill it with natural things; for which they find little or no relief. Some build massive corporations, businesses, and establishments, trying to fill that unexplained yearning inside of them; a yearning that is both spiritual and natural; spiritual, because of his God-self, and natural because of his divine calling to have dominion over everything.

Genesis says three specific things of the created man:

1. He is made in God's image.
2. He is made after God's likeness.
3. He was to have dominion over everything upon the earth.

In other words, man was supposed to rule everything upon the earth because he is "the god" in God's place upon the earth. Man is the only creature created to represent the Creator.

To fully understand himself, man must first take a good look at God, and understand Him. First, God is one of faith; He operates and drives upon the hymnals of faith-He declares it, and it comes to pass.

In Genesis, chapter one, it reads that "God said" nine times, and after God says it, the next few verses declares that it was so, or that it came to pass. God is a God that operates by faith. He says it and it comes to pass.

Thus, man is firstly a creature of faith; that's why it is paramount that you are careful of your speech and what comes out of your mouth. You are God's child. You contain the power and character of God, your creator. He made you to be just like Him, so every word that comes out of your mouth is filled with power. Solomon tried to explain this principle to us when he penned Proverbs 18: 20-21. Note what he says:

20. A man's belly shall be satisfied with the fruit of his mouth and with the increase of his lips shall he be filled.

21. Death and life are in the power of the tongue: and they that love it shall eat the fruit thereof.

Just like God, whatever we say has power! It destroys or gives life. We are God children. The Light of God resides in us, and if we are not learned of the power and light of God in us, it works against us.

When Solomon says that a man's belly shall be satisfied by the fruit of his mouth, he means that a man's needs shall be met by the words that come out of his mouth. As children of God, the entire cosmos brings to you what you declare from your mouth, even if it works against you. If you declare it, it comes to pass. The universe obeys you because you are the children of the Most High God dwelling upon the earth.

Most men do not realize the light of God rests in them.

Now I know that this statement will startle you, but we are all gods because we are the children of God. But, most of us will descend the grave as mere men-never realizing their true identity. Note what the book of psalms says of this matter. Psalms 82: 5-7:

5. They know not, neither will they understand ; they walk on in darkness: all the foundations of the earth are out of course.
6. I have said, you are gods; and all of you are children of the most High.
7. But you shall die like men, and fall like one of te princes.

Look at what the Psalmist says; we are gods because we are the children of the Most High God. But look what he says; even though we are gods, we shall die as mere men. This is because most of us will never come to fully realize our god-self.

For the Psalmist to say the "But" you shall die as mere men, suggest that we are not supposed to die as mere men, but as "godmen" that walked and lived as the children of the most High God.

Note what Jesus says about the matter of our words. Matthew 12: 36-37:

36. But I say unto you. That every idle word that men shall speak, they shall give account thereof in the Day of Judgment.

37. For by your words you shall be justified, and by your words you shall be condemned.

In other words, Jesus was saying that our every word affects our lives. Our words do just what we say-even when we don't mean them to.

We are God's spirit encapsulated by flesh and endowed with a soul. There are three parts to the god-man upon the earth. He has a body, a soul, and a spirit. His body is taken from the earth. It is dissolving daily-he is gradually dying every day because his body is of the earth (God designed that all earthly things must soon die); He has a soul, which is his intellect; that for which he learns as he sojourns upon the earth. The longer he lives upon earth, the larger his soul becomes. Lastly, man has a spirit-the spirit of God-the light of God. It never dies. It is released upon the death of the body. The body cannot live without the spirit, but the spirit will live on without the body.

His body gives him the ability to speak, taste, feel, smell, "experience", the things upon the earth. His soul gives him the ability to think and reason, and his spirit is that which keeps him connected to God, his Father and creator.

Because man lives in a world filled with taste, feelings, smell, hearing, and a host of experiences, he rations and acknowledges only the physical aspect of himself; and there are few to teach him other-wise because he is surrounded by others who are confined to the earthly. We can only teach that for which we have been taught.

We carry "the light" of God in us, but nobody taught us of the light. So, we die before we ever truly live and understand just "who" we really are. Man dies before he physically dies because he never lives the life that he was created to live. He lives in a surreptitious state of being, for who he is, is even hidden from he himself, and the most unfortunate thing is, is that he will never serendipitously wonder into himself.

To die, by definition, means to cease to exist, so thus, when we take a panoramic look at man, he is living while dead; for to him the light in him is non sub sequential, therefore, he experience consequential damages because of his endowed ignorance.

God designated us as keepers of the light. To not know the light, is to live in darkness. Man innately knows that; his spirit man cries out to his creator; that's the reason why he builds buildings with steeples, and rush therein hoping to find the presence of God, his creator-not realizing that he carries his creator inside of him. So then, the steeple building becomes a subconscious decadent reminder of his failed self.

Because I am the keeper of the light, I have the power of God in me, so that I am just like Him. I am Him in flesh; therefore, nothing is impossible for me. I create my own reality and maintain and sustain my own destiny. My reality is what I choose it to be-bad or good. I determine who I am, and who I shall come to be. There is no greater force on earth than I. No other creature is equal or parallel to me; for I am the only one of His creatures that He put some of Himself in, and enveloped me with His power.

The only power that my enemy has over me is the power that I have given them. This is what Jesus was trying to tell KING Pilate when He told Pilate that he had no power over Him. Note John 19: 10-11:

10. Then said Pilate unto him, speak you not unto me? Know you not that I have power to crucify you, and have power to release you?
11. Jesus answered, You could have no power at all against me, except it were given you from above.

So thus, I hold my own destiny in my hands. It is what I choose it to be.

You are more than a mere mortal man. You are the keeper of the light of God. It rests on the inside of you.

The light is so powerful that mortal words cannot explain it or describe it. You have been chosen to keep the light until the day that your flesh dies and returns back to the earth. The light then leaves your flesh and returns back to God where it truly exists.

If you should ever realize the light in you, you shall be a force to be reckoned with.

No earthly position, title, place, or people can define you, or give you definition, or purpose. You do that entirely by yourself. Even failing to be something, you inadvertently choose to be nothing, but you're not entirely "nothing", for the light of God still rests in you.

CHAPTER TWO

A PRIVILEGED PURPOSE

F irstly, in order to walk in your true destiny, you've got to realize how truly blessed and privileged you are, and I underscore "privileged", to understand this you must digest Genesis 1: 28; note what it says:

And God blessed them, and God said unto them, Be fruitful, and multiply, and replenish the earth, and subdue it: and have dominion over the fish of the sea, and over the fowl of the air, and over every living thing that moves upon the earth.

At some point in previous times, before "we" were created, God had created another generation of mankind. How many others He created before us, we shall never know; or why He chose to destroy them, we also do not know, but what is apparently crystal clear is that He chose to create another generation of mankind, which is where we come in.

I say that we are the privileged ones because, simply put, He could have chosen not to create another man all together. I choose to believe that, like present man, the previous creations, failed to know and acknowledge who they were, thus, their demise.

No other animal created, or plant, or any such thing can boast of our identity, or suggest even a remote parallel to God; only the privileged man that He chose to created-again.

Now, as you will read in the book of Genesis out of the King James Bible, man's purpose is to reproduce others as himself-"Be fruitful and multiply". This does not mean to just have babies and fill the earth ; no, rather, to reproduce off-springs that will honor God and keep the light. But, Adam failed to teach his son Abel; and Abraham failed to teach his son Isaac, and Isaac failed to teach his son Jacob, and so on and so forth right down to this very present age. One cannot teach that for which one does not know.

Adam got so caught-up in his newly love affair with the freshly created woman that God had made for him, until he forgot to teach her and his sons the authentic purpose of why God had created them.

The most prevalent thing that Adam passed on to us is the passion for love and romance, and a deep quest to acquire "things". We learned to value who we are by how much material stuff that we can acquire. Our purpose becomes lost amongst the things that we have acquired during our lives, or shall we say during the time of our lack of real living.

Our true purpose was and still is to let His glory shine forth into the earth through us-the significant part of His creation.

Because of our lack of honoring Him, and allowing His glory and essence to flow through us, we become the best of God's creation and at the very same time, we become the worst of His creation. It is a paradox.

Because man is incognizant of who he is, and how very privileged he is, he, without ever thinking, embraces all of his frailties. He becomes subject to that for which he was supposed to rule.

A slave cannot teach another slave how to be free, and it is most difficult to give a slave freedom if he does not first realize that he is, in fact, a slave.

CHAPTER THREE

THE LIGHT

Y ou are the possessor of the powerful thing known to man, or shall we say unknown to man. The light in you, which is God's glory, rests in your bosom. It contains more power than anything known to man, or anything that was created.

The light that you possess has more power than the natural light that your eyes can behold. Scientist estimate that natural light travels at 186,282 miles per second- almost 700,000,000 mph. Can you ever imagine that? But, the light in you, the light given you from God is, by far, more powerful than that.

If you should look up into the sky at noon day, during the fullness of the sun, you still wouldn't even get a glimpse of the power of the light in you.

Because of the light that you carry in your bosom, nothing is impossible to you; no, nothing. God explains this to us in the book of Genesis 11: 4-7. Note what it says:

4. And they said, "Come, let us build ourselves a city, and a tower whose top is in the heavens: let us make a name for ourselves, lest we be scattered abroad over the face of the whole earth.":

5. But the Lord came down to see the city and the tower which the sons of men had built.

6. And the Lord said, "Indeed the people are one and they all have one language, and this is what they begin to do; now nothing that they propose to do will be withheld from them.

7. "Come, let Us go down and there confuse their language. That they may not understand one another's speech."

Understand that God said that if they speak the same language, that nothing is impossible for them-nothing! He wasn't just alluding to the fact that they spoke the same language; no, it was because of the Light that they possessed inside of them "and" and ability to communicate as one. They could do anything – just as their creator, who is the God that speaks things into existence. He says, "Let there be" and it becomes.

Note what Jesus says of man carrying the light; Matthew 5: 14-16:

14. You are the light of the world. A city that is set on an hill cannot be hid.

15. Neither do men light a candle, and put it under a bushel, but on a candle stick; and it gives light unto all that are in the house.
16. Let your light so shine before men, that they may see your good works, and glorify your Father which is in heaven.

Jesus was saying that "we are" the light; we are the possessors of the light; therefore, we should guide men to the knowledge of the light that is in them.

Look what He says about our light in John 8: 12:

12. Then spoke Jesus again unto them, saying, I am the light of the world; he that follows me shall not walk in darkness, but shall have the light of light.

When one surmises the whole of Jesus, the end result is that He was sent to remind mankind of his real true self-the light bearer.

Before Jehovah created man, according to the book of Genesis account, the world and the entire cosmos was engulfed in darkness. The very first thing that Jehovah does is speak light into existence-the bible said that God said let there be light, and there was light; this was before He created the sun and the moon, so it had to be a different kind of light; the same light source that abides inside of us; the light that we bear.

This brilliant, all engulfing light resides in us to enable us to accomplish that for which we were created to do-glorify of God in our every action.

The gives us unlimited boundaries; nothing is impossible for us.

Observe what the Apostle Paul says about this light that we possess. Romans 13: 11-12:

11. And that, knowing the time, that now it is high time to awake out of sleep: for now is our salvation nearer than when we believed.
12. The night is far spent, the day is at hand: let us therefore cast off the works of darkness, and let us put on the armor of light.

The Apostle Paul was saying that we have wasted enough time in darkness-not embracing the light, and fighting with the light.

Resting in our bosom is something more powerful than any mega bomb; more powerful than the splitting of the atom to make a nuclear weapon. It is the light; the essence of God- The part that makes the hu-man godly.

Without the light inside of man, he becomes just a lifeless hunk of clay. The is what gives him the ability to become animated. Others have called that which gives man life, the breath of God, but God, Jehovah calls it the light.

King David even said that God's Word also bears the light, for its light guides men to The Light. Notice what King David states in Psalms 119: 105:

Your word is a lamp unto my feet, and a light unto my path.

In other words, what king David was saying was that God's word is a light that will give you awareness of the light.

Jehovah made you out of light; that is why without light you cease to exist. Man is more light than he is flesh, for his flesh is only a vessel designed to carry the light.

God's secret place is inside of every man. It's a secret because nobody taught the masses of men who they are and what their purpose is. The secret is hid right in plain view. He lies down with it, walk with it, eats with it. Everything that he does is with the light; he is just ignorant of the light, so thus, it is, ironically hid from him right in plain sight-inside of him. He couldn't get rid of the light if he truly wanted to.

Many times the reason why man fails to possess the light is because of the company that he surrounds himself with. You see, one can never become an eagle if all that he surrounds himself with are sparrows. He will take on the nature of the sparrow.

The Apostle Paul says that part of the reason why men fail to walk in the light of their true identity is because of the company that they keep. You cannot learn to see while being taught by the blind. Jesus said that the blind cannot lead the blind because they both will fall into a ditch. You will never become higher than the ones that you often keep company with; usually, your company will coerce you to embellish your present state-even when it is not to your best interest.

It is the classes concept-people generally migrate to the class that is most like them, the ones that makes them feel most comfortable in who they are. This class concept is the reason why man can never have true democracy (Democracy sounds good, but it is only make-believe at best), because the classes will always be for their own kind-hence, they are automatically aloof and ambivalent towards those of a different class. The Apostle Paul warns us of this situation. Observe:

Ephesians 5: 6-8 says:

6. Let no man deceive you with vain words: for because of these things comes the wrath of God upon the children of disobedience.
7. Be not you therefore partakers with them.
8. For you were sometimes darkness, but now are you light in the Lord: walk as children of light.

In order for you to "be" the light that you were created to be, you must be taught by someone that is already cognizant of the light. Look what the Apostle Paul says. He says that you are the light-not you carry the light, but rather, the light is you. That's why you cannot be defeated, or overthrown, or belittled, because you are the light, and all the privileges and power and might of God is in you right now. It is no wonder that the prophet Isaiah said that no weapon formed against you shall prosper-**YOU ARE THE LIGHT!!!!!!**

Light disperses all darkness, and unveils the impurities surrounding us. It awakens mans subconscious mind to things he had previously failed to see.

Angel of light

Because the devil knows that we are children of light, he tries to deceive us by disguising himself as an angel of light. Note what the Apostle Paul says of Satan in 2 Corinthians 11: 14:

And no wonder! For Satan himself transforms himself into an angel of light.

He wants to deceive us by immolating who we are-children of light.

The devil is referred to as a deceiver because the only power that he has over us is the power that we give him; which is the reason why he tries to bring fear to us.

Man's greatest misfortune is that he rarely realizes that he is the keeper of the light, thus he usually dies defeated.

When you realize that you carry the light of The Almighty God in your bosom, you then become exposed to the power and purpose of the light.

I am often amazed by how much ignorance pervades many local churches. They seek God in the pews; so thus, they adamantly search for and desire "a feeling", which they often get, but they have "a feeling" but no power..........dancing in defeat.

We are the light, and because of that, **WE CANNOT BE DEFEATED!!!!** We can't even die-as we know death to be. We are simply transformed from one life to another. Paul was referring to this principal when he penned I Corinthians 15: 53-55:

53. For this corruptible must put on incorruption, and this mortal must put on immortality.
54. So when this corruptible shall have put on incorruption, and this mortal shall have put on immortality, then shall be brought to pass the saying that is written, Death is swallowed up in victory.
55. O death, where is your sting? O grave, where is your victory?

You are the keeper of the light, but you have to choose to walk in victory. You have to choose not to be defeated. You must choose to overcome; this is not based upon a feeling, but a declaration from God.

I am the strength and breathe of Jehovah even when I don't feel like it. I walk in the light because I am the light.

This is what Jesus was referring to when He said, "Walk in the light."

Because our prophets (preachers) have little or no understanding of the light, they become just dispensers of enticing words through feel good sermons filled with motivation speeches.

You must repeat these phases daily until it becomes a part of you; until you become what you say that you are. The power is in your words.

I am the keeper of the light; I am the light; I represent the supreme God Jehovah in my beliefs and therefore through my actions. I walk in victory daily. The light fills me with power from heaven to live as I was created to live......In prosperity, in health, in wellness, in peace, and in soundness of mind.

CHAPTER FOUR

THE POWER OF WORSHIP

To know and understand God, you must know and understand your purpose. **Purpose** is the reason **"why"** you were created, or better still, for what reason did God create you?

In Genesis the first chapter, we notice that God made man, a part of His creation, after he had finished making everything else. This is very important to understand! After He had finished making all else, the sun, the moon, the stars, the trees, the animals… etc, Jehovah then created man.

Man, the last of God's creation, first purpose is to take care of what God had created upon the earth; that is why He gave him dominion over everything. This introduces us to God's natural and spiritual law-in order to operate upon the earth, you must inhabit flesh.

The reason why the devil tries to possess people is because he has to abide by God's natural and spiritual law for the earth-you have to have flesh to experience the things on the earth. Man is flesh and spirit. The devil is spirit that wants flesh.

So, man's first purpose is to take care of what God had created upon the earth.

Man's last and second purpose is to **worship God.** Well, exactly what is worship? Worship is to show reverence and adoration for God. It is to honor God. Worship is the sole purpose of our religious service.

So hence, worship service is a time that we come together to collectively show adoration for our God through song, sermon, dance, and the lifting up to heaven our hands.

There is great power in our worship; for worship gets God's attention and moves Him faster than anything else. Worship is the time when we come together to praise God.

David, in the book of Psalms, gives us a glimpse of what our worship service should be like. Note Psalms 150: 1-6:

1. Praise you the Lord. Praise God in his sanctuary: praise him in the firmament of his power.
2. Praise him for his mighty acts: praise him according to his excellent greatness.
3. Praise him with the sound of the trumpet: praise him with the psaltery and harp.

4. Praise him with stringed instruments and organs.
5. Praise him upon the loud cymbals: praise him upon the high sounding cymbals.
6. Let everything that has breath praise the Lord. Praise you the Lord.

David emphasizes the importance of our worship through praise. Note, there is great expression through our worshipping him.

It is important to note that if your worship does not move you, then it certainly does not move God and heaven; to the degree that your worship and praise moves you, is the same degree in which it moves God.

Sometimes our worship must get radical with loud singing and great expressions and dancing, yes, dancing. Observe what David says of worship and dance in Psalms 149: 3:

Let them praise his name in the dance: let them sing unto him with the timbrel and harp.

Yes, he said dance in our worship service. Remember, worship is our showing adoration for our God. It is being thankful unto him.

David instructs us to dance from his own experience. Note what 2 Samuel 6: 14 says:

And David danced before the Lord with all his might; and David was girded with a linen ephod.

CHAPTER FIVE

UNDERSTANDING THE DEPTH OF YOUR SOUL

The other night, I lay upon my bed in the pitch darkness of night as the light from the moon eased through my drape adorned window. God spoke softly to me, and said unto me, "Do you know the depth of your soul?"

I pondered for a moment, and then said, "No."

He whispered to me, "Close your eyes."

I did, but I saw nothing but utter darkness. "I see nothing." I said.

"But you see everything in that nothing that you see."

I didn't understand.

And then, God explained to me the essence of my soul, and what it encompasses.

God explained to me that when I closed my eyes, I saw the darkness and depth of the whole universe right there inside of me. I was connected to it without ever even realizing it. My soul was a part of it. I have no bottom or top, or width. The whole of me is immeasurable. I am a spiritual black whole taken from Jehovah the Father.

Out of me, comes forth the whole of mankind; out of me, comes the purpose of my creator and His creation; hidden right inside of me. Everything that had ever been, and everything that shall ever be was right inside of me, just as it was when I gazed up into the night sky-the whole of God's creation looks back at me. The past, the future, and the present dwelled in the night sky and rested inside of me.

When my flesh dies, the whole of me is released back to the whole of Jehovah's creation-the creature returns to the creation.

It is like the banana; while it looks good on the outside, the best part is on the inside-after you peel it. We spend a life time treasuring the outside of ourselves, and forget the inside.

The Chinese calls it Zen. The Koreans calls it Chi. It is that invisible part of you that dwells on the inside of you. The part of you that cannot be quenched, stopped, or contained by outside forces.

When Jesus said that all things are possible to you, He meant that when you connect with your inner self; your God self, there are no impossibilities for you. You, in fact become a supernatural being.

Your power comes from within you! You cannot see it; you cannot touch it, but you can feel it when you become acquainted with the feel of its indwelling power racing though your terrestrial veins.

So thus, is the reason why you are what you say that you are, and you become whatever you believe that you shall become-good or bad; that is why you have to be taught how to tap into your inner God self.

The scriptures say that God cannot lie. Whatever He says is always truth. If God looks at a wall, and says that there is no wall, then that very wall shall disappear. Whatever God says, comes to pass. There is no contrary.

You are in the image of God encapsulated by flesh. There is absolute power in your words. When they leave your lips, they search for paths to bring to pass whatever you have spoken.

Note what Jesus says in Matthew 12:37:

For by your words you will be justified, and by your words you will be condemned.

Everything hinges upon your words; the things that comes out of your mouth.

I cannot stress the importance that words coming out of your mouth play in your life. Our entire lives are built upon what has been proceeding out of our mouths.

If things are not going well with you, tap into your inner self-the real you, where God resides-your soul.

There are cultures and people that spend most of their time becoming in tuned with their soul. The Shaolin monks of China could do supernatural things with their bodies because they spent most of their days developing their inward soul. Their bodies responded to their soul's request, therefore they were able to do things that defied physical limitations.

The soul controls every single thing around it; right down to a very single grain of sand.

Jesus said that God is connected to everything. Observe what He says in Matthew 10:29:

But not a single sparrow can fall to the ground without your Father knowing it

Jesus says this to show how your creator is connected to everything. The reason why He uses the sparrow in this illustration is because the sparrow is a very plenteous bird; there are perhaps billions of them, but if one of them, of that billion, falls to the ground, God knows of it. So often times we miss Jesus ultimate point because we merely focus on God taking care of our physical needs, but this far supersedes just caring for our physical needs. It illustrates the all knowing, all seeing, and all power of the Creator being connected to the creatures.

It is not the ceasing of the sparrow's wings to flap. It is the sparrow becoming disconnected to The Source.

Now if the little numerous sparrow is connected to God, and God cares for it, imagine how much more God cares for you who are made in His image and His likeness.

The reason why the enemy tries to get you to focus on everything, and material gain is because he doesn't ever wants you to realize where your true strength and worth lies.

Over and over again and again, Jesus illustrates the depth of our souls and the power than we harness. Note, in the bible, Mark 4:37-41:

37. And there arose a great storm of wind, and the waves beat into the ship, so that it was now full.
38. And He was in the hinder part of the ship, asleep on a pillow; and they awake him, and say unto him, Master, care you not that we perish?
39. And he arose, and rebuked the wind, and said unto the sea, Peace be still. And the wind ceased, and there was a great calm.
40. And he said unto them, Why are you so fearful? How is it that you have no faith?
41. And they feared exceedingly, and said one to another, What manner of man is this, that even the wind and the sea obey him?

When the disciples asked, "What manner of man is this?" They were literally asking each other, what "kind" of man is this.

He can speak, and the elements obey Him. Yes, because His inner soul, like yours, is connected to everything in the universe. So, the lesser element, the inanimate, obey Him.

Jehovah took the greater part of the universe and placed it deep inside of man, His creation.

Inside of you, is an endless black hole of knowledge, power, and wealth; and when you realize and understand this, you shall then understand that everything on the outside of you is merely designed for creature comfort.

A chair is merely a chair; a car is merely a car; a house, no matter how large it is, is merely a house, and a job, no matter how much it pays, is merely a job-or career. They are all creature comforts. They were never designed to enhance your worth as a Being, only to give you a degree of comfort while you sojourn on your way to becoming a part of the great celestial-where you came from.

But, nobody taught you this, and nobody taught your parents this, and nobody taught your great parents this, so you simply immolated your parents just as they had immolated their parents-deciding that self worth had to be somehow connected to what material gain you come to have in this life.

Allow me to illustrate this point. Booker T. Washington said that when he first came to the south to teach, he went from house to house, or shack to shack, meeting the different people-many of them ex-slaves. He said that what he noticed, in most of their houses, were a piano, but nobody in the family could play the piano.

They didn't have ample silverware, plates, forks, spoons etc; neither ample furniture, but most had a piano crammed somewhere in their house. Why, because they equated the piano with self worth and wealth: that's what they had seen in most of the white folks big plantation houses.

This image of wealth is the reason why most drive cars that they cannot afford; live in houses that they cannot afford, and buy clothes that they cannot afford.

The devil tried to get Jesus to succumb to that image of wealth. Matthew 4: 8-9:

8. Again the devil takes him up into an exceedingly high mountain, and shows him all the kingdoms of the world, and the glory of them;
9. And says unto him, All these things will I give you if you will fall down and worship me.

You see he knew that Jesus had something on the inside of him that was richer and more powerful than anything on the outside of him. He already knew that because of His inside, he already owned everything on the outside. The devil hoped that Jesus didn't already know his true worth.

Jesus also stressed the importance of prioritizing true wealth. Note what He says to His disciples in Matthew 6:31-33:

31. Therefore take no thought, saying, What shall we eat? Or, what shall we drink? Or, how shall we be clothed?
32. (For after all these things do the Gentiles seek;) For your heavenly Father knows you have need of all these thing.
33. But seek you God, and his righteousness, and all these other things shall be added unto you.

Jesus is saying that if you put God first and focus on your soul, the deeper inside of you, God will supply all of your needs; and notice that He parenthesized that all these things do the Gentiles seek.

Gentile, is somebody that does not know Jehovah God and those not have a relationship with Him, thus, not knowing that He dwells on the inside of them, so they seek wealth and self worth through things and material stuff.

They chase that image of wealth, while their real wealth goes forsaken.

It is seemingly a paradox; for when you value the inside of you-the soul, the outside becomes less valued. When you realize, and harness the power of your soul inside of you, then you can have whatever is outside of you, but when you grasp your soul, those things outside of you are less important-thus, the paradox. When I can truly have it, I don't want it.

My soul is deeper than the deepest ocean; it is more vast than the entire universe; there-in lies the reason why I cannot be destroyed. I can only be altered from one degree of life to another. I am as my creator is. I am, my soul is, connected to Jehovah-the most high and supreme God of all creation, and all that is, and all that ever was, and all that shall come to be. I am a connected part of the whole-my soul.

CHAPTER SIX

IN TUNED WITH YOUR SOUL

There are at least ten essential things that you must be prepared to practice daily. These seven things will thrust you forward into a deeper more in-depth reality to your true self, and enhance your relationship with your creator-Jehovah. Note the seven practices (we say practice because you must routinely do them).

1. Reading
2. Writing
3. Meditation
4. Change
5. Growth
6. Prayer
7. Pain
8. Rehearse
9. Encourage
10. Language

The list could include more, but if you will practice these things, you will evolve into the god-man (man here is not gender specific) that you were designed to be.

Just observing your natural self, you were designed to grow and become stronger and more vibrant; not to become brittle and fragile with old age. Growing older is what "you" design it to be.

Observe what the bible says about Moses and him growing older:

Deuteronomy 34: 7:
And Moses was an hundred and twenty years old when he died: his eye was not dim, nor his natural force abated.

That is saying that Moses, at 120 years old, still had good eye sight and he did not suffer with the side effects of growing old-that what it means when it says that his natural force did not abate-he didn't act old, look or feel old.

It was not a natural occurrence; Moses chose what his condition would be. In Genesis 27: 1, it states that Isaac suffered from old age-his eyes were dim. When you read Genesis 48: 10, it talks of Jacob (Israel) eyes being dim-old age.

Moses didn't suffer from getting older because he chose not to. I believe that he, no doubt, did some of, if not all of, the afore mentioned ten practices we ascribed.

Another case in point, Joshua 14: 10-12:

10. And now, behold, the Lord has kept me alive, as he said, these forty and five years, even since the Lord spoke this word unto Moses, while the children of Israel wondered in the wilderness; and now, lo, I am this day fourscore and five years old.
11. As yet I am as strong this day as I was in the day that Moses sent me: as my strength was then, even so is my strength now, for war, both to go out, and to come in.
12. Now therefore give me this mountain, whereof the Lord spoke in that day; for you heard in that day how the Anakims were there, and that the cities were great and fenced: if so be the lord will be with me, then I shall be able to drive them out, as the Lord said.

Note, Caleb declared that he was, at 85 years old, as strong as he was at 45 years old. He chose to keep his strength and not suffer from the usual effects of natural old age.

Again, I believe that in some form Caleb applied the ten practices that we listed earlier.

Let us observe the ten disciplines more closely of getting in tuned with your soul:

1. **Reading**: You must spend great time reading the Holy Word of God-the bible, and any and all books that relate to righteous living, or living right. The more that you read, the more your mind expands and become knowledgeable to the things of Jehovah. Don't restrict yourself to just reading the bible or only things that deal with religion, but rather delve into all literature-science, the arts, psychology, astrology, etc, because at the end of the day, all will point back to Jehovah. Remember, the more that you read, the more that you expand your conscious and subconscious being. It is like eating. You cannot remain strong

and able to do work to accomplish things if you don't first supply your body with nutrients. Reading is spiritual nutrition for you. Read the Torah and learn how Moses was able to remain faithful during all of his times of testing; learn how was Joshua able to keep his youthful strength even at 85 years old, and learn how Abraham pleased God so until he was called a friend of God. You can only acquire a strong grip in this knowledge by reading those texts for yourself. The more that you read, the more that you grow. It enables you to be able to pour into others lives. Look at what Jesus says about pouring into others: John 7: 37-38: In the last day, that great day of the feast, Jesus stood, and cried, saying, If any man thirst, let him come after me, and drink. He that believes on me, as the scripture has said, out of his belly shall flow rivers of living water...............In other words, somebody should be drinking from your well, but they cannot if you don't fill it first. Reading helps fill your well of knowledge, so that you can pour into others.

2. **Writing**: Writing things down, helps you to retain it, and when you retain it, you can pull it back up again when needed. It is so essential to write things down. Note God telling the prophet to write his vision down so that it would be plain for the people. Habakkuk 2:2: And the lord answered me, and said, Write the vision, and make it plain upon tables, that he may run that reads it. When we write it, it sticks with us. And also, writing gives you the ability to share your experience with someone else even in your absence. When your intellect has slipped and forgotten, the written word will produce it again unto you.

3. **Meditation**: The definition of meditation is, to think deeply or focus one's mind in silence upon something. It is paramount that we set aside some time each day to meditate upon Jehovah-to hear from God. It is very difficult to hear from God during the havoc of your busy days. No, you must set aside some quiet time that you might focus your attention without diversion. In the bible, in the book of 1 Kings, observe what it says about the voice of God: 1 Kings 19: 11-12: And he said, Go forth, and stand upon the mount before the Lord. And, behold, the Lord

passed by, and great and strong ind rent the mountains, and broke in pieces the rocks before the Lord; but the Lord was not in the wind: and after the wind an earthquake; but the Lord was not in the earthquake: 12. And after the earthquake a fire; but the Lord was not in the fire: and after the fire a still small voice………….Note, God spoke in a small still voice; that is a soft whisper, which is the reason why one must meditate, it is quite difficult to hear and understand a whisper when one is in the midst of a crowd or confusion. No, you must set aside some quiet time that you can focus on what the Lord is saying to you. He is still speaking to you, sometimes daily, but you cannot hear Him unless you are focusing quietly on Him. Turn your T.V, your cell phone, your radio, and whatever other gadgets that you might have that will interrupt you, turn them off and sit or lie in a quiet place and listen for God's voice and God's instruction.

4. **Change**: The willingness to change and accept changes are so important to you being in tuned with your soul, and becoming the power riddled being that God designed you to be. In order to grow, you must being willing to change. Growth will never occur without change. You must expect change. Sometimes change difficult because so often we are not ready or prepared for it, but it is essential to your spiritual growth. It is like Moses going through change. He lived to be 120 years old, but his life was divided into three major changes consisting of 40 years each-40 years as a prince in Pharaoh's castle; 40 years as a shepherd in the mountains, and 40 years a prophet to delivered God's people to the Promised Land. Change helps to prepare us for our destiny. You cannot achieve your destiny and understand the true essence of your soul, without change.

5. **Growth**: This would seem needless to discuss, but spiritual growth does not just automatically comes. Unlike physical growth, you must choose to grow spiritually; and just going to church does not propel you to grow. When you do all the other steps in this book, you are choosing to grow; and by picking up this book and reading it, is an indication that you are choosing

to grow. It is in reading, meditation, worship, writing, and praying. Do these and watch yourself grow to higher heights.

6. **Prayer:** Of all the soul building disciplines that I have spoken of here-to-fore, prayer is the most essential; for the literal meaning of prayer is to have conversation with God-to talk to God and listen to Him talk to you. It is not just when you get on your knees and say some kind of religious recital. Prayer is also not restricted to where you are, whether in a church, or on a bus, or standing on the street corner. Unlike what most people think, prayer is usually done inaudible. The Apostle Paul says in 1 Thessalonians 5: 16-17: Rejoice evermore. Pray without ceasing. ……….. How can one pray none stop-because prayer is a spiritual conversation with God; often times silently within yourself. Paul says rejoice always through prayer. So often many people simply talk to God, but after you talk to Him, you've got to wait and allow Him to talk back to you-wait for an answer; sometimes He says yes; sometimes He says no; sometimes He says maybe, and other times He says wait. You must converse with Him. Daniel made it through the night in the lion's den because he spent the night talking with God. We gain spiritual depth through prayer. When you note the life of Jesus, you see that He spends a great deal of time in prayer. He prayed, and something happened; He prayed, and something happened; He prayed, and something happened. This happens over and over again. Jesus talks to the Father, and then a miracle happens. If we want to see more miracles in our lives, we have got to spend more time in prayer. The heart of God resides in our soul-inside of us. Notice what God says about blessings and prayer in the book of Isaiah. Isaiah 65: 23-24: They shall not labor in vain, nor bring forth for trouble; for they are the seed of the blessed of the Lord, and their offspring with them. And it shall come to pass, that before they call, I ill answer; and while they are yet speaking, I will hear……….What the book of Isaiah is saying is that you are blessed because you can talk to God, and He talks back to you. He says that you don't have to always wait for an answer; he says that sometimes He will answer you while you

are yet calling. You should talk to God more that you talk to anybody.

7. **Pain:** In order to properly grow spiritually, you've got to go through a degree of pain, just as your physical body does not grow without pain. Pain equals discomfort, but it is so very necessary for your maturity. If you do not experience some pain and discomfort in your life and ministry, then, I can assure you that you are not growing too much. Pain makes us move forward, and fix what is wrong. It is the way that our bodies work. When we experience pain, we know that something is wrong. Through pain, our bodies are screaming to us that something is wrong and needs our attention-the greater the pain, the more severe the situation. A leader must anticipate some pain in ranks. So, if you are experiencing discomfort, do not be discouraged, God will give you the strength to make it through your pain; and know that it is designed to force you to become better spiritually and physically.

8. **Rehearse:** Now rehearse simply means "Practice"- to perform over and over again, seeking perfection in the act. Practice meditation. Practice your prayer life. Do it over and over again until it becomes a part of you. Rehearse walking in the fullness of the God Head. The more that you rehearse your true identity, the easier it becomes to be the God man that Jehovah created you to me. When you first start to meditate, your mind will probably go a thousand other places, but you must continue to practice meditation until you are able to easily ease into to that place of peace where you can calmly commune with God.

9. **Encourage:** This is to give support to someone to continue onward in their endeavors, but it is not to just give encouragement to someone else; sometimes you've got to encourage yourself. Many times, the only support system that you will have will be your own self. King David had come to such a place when all of his family and his soldiers 'families had been taken captive by an enemy. All the men blamed King David, and wanted to kill him; but, during this time, with no one supporting him, King David encouraged himself. Observe what 1 Samuel 30: 6: And

David was greatly distressed; for the people spoke of stoning him, because the soul of all the people as grieved, every man for his sons and for his daughters: but David encouraged himself in the Lord his God...................You have got to encourage yourself to perform these ten disciplines for spiritual growth, and getting in touch with your inward man-your soul. Note what Ephesians 5: 19 says: Speaking to yourselves in psalms and hymns and spiritual songs, singing and making melody in your heart to the Lord..Paul said sing to yourself to encourage yourself in your endeavors. When you feel alone, and perhaps feel like you are failing, know that you are not alone. God is right where you are. Don't stop at just encouraging yourself, but encourage others also, for whatever you put out, the same returns unto you.

10. **Language:** Your method of communication is your language-The method in which you use to convey your thoughts. It is "how" you say what you are saying; it is "when" you say what you are saying, and how much conviction and faith are in what you are saying. It boils down to speaking with authority. There is a distinct difference in how a peasant communicates, and how a king and his children communicate. Notice in the bible how it says that Jesus spoke. Look at what by-standers said about His language. Matthew 7: 28-29.......And it came to pass, when Jesus had ended these sayings, the people were astonished at his doctrine: For he taught them as one having authority, and not as the scribes........................Your language must be that of an heir; one of God's children that walks in entitlement. You cannot do this unless you have a firm belief in "who" you are in God. Your language must be that which propels genuine authority. When we believe and use the right language, the devil and the whole universe has to get in accord with what we have spoken, but we must speak with conviction and authority. We must believe that what we are saying shall come to pass. Observe the power that Jesus' disciples had. Luke 10: 17: And the seventy returned again with joy, saying, Lord, even the devils are subject unto us through your name................................This

kind of authoritative language is not available to immature children of God. Your relationship with Jehovah is a growing one. You must be developed, and that can only come with time-growth requires time. Christianity is a growing process; you are constantly under construction. God is continuously working with you and on you to produce a "God man" that is in the image of Himself. **YOU HAVE TO CHOOSE TO GROW!!!!!** Why, because look at what the Apostle Paul says to us in the book of Galatians 4: 1: Now I say, That the heir, as long as he is a child, differs nothing from a servant, though he be lord of all.......................What Paul is saying is that even though everything belongs to you, and you are God's heir, you are no more than a servant until you grow up in Him and learn what you possess and the power that is in your hand, or else you will be more destructive than productive-even to your own self.

Your language has to be one of authority, and your daily living must match your language, or else your living will cancel out what you are saying. The devil will constantly try to tempt you to mere human character. His first temptation of Jesus was to see if Jesus knew who he really was-was He aware of His God-ship. Matthew 4: 5-6: Then the devil takes him up into the holy city, and sits him on a pinnacle of the temple, 6. And says unto him, If you be the Son of God, cast yourself down; for it is written, He shall give his angels charge concerning you; and in their hands they shall bear you up, lest at any time you dash your foot against a stone.........The devil was quoting scripture (Psalms 91) to Jesus to see if he knew and understood the power that He already possess from God the Father. And, you will note that in those same verses of scripture, Jesus proved conclusively that He knew "who" He was and the power that He possessed. Your language must be one of authority through the power of Jehovah.

The afore mentioned ten steps will ensure your becoming and remaining in tuned with your soul-the deeper part of you where your real power lies.

CHAPTER SEVEN

GOD'S SECRET PLACE

Psalms 91: 1-3:

1. **He that dwells in the secret place of the most High shall abide under the shadow of the Almighty.**
2. **I will say of the Lord, He is my refuge and my fortress: my God; in him will I trust.**
3. **Surely he shall deliver you from the snare of the fowler, and from the noisome pestilence.**

King David is saying that when you find God's secret place, you have found a place of peace and confident resolve. God's secret place promises five things: 1. Access to the power of the Almighty. 2. A place to retire. 3. A place of protection. 4. A guard against your enemies. 5. Health and wellness of body and soul.

We must seek to find God's secret place, where we can evolve to become what we were created to be. We were created to walk in God's power, God's protection, and enjoy God's given health and wellness. Remember, we were never designed to experience old age. We were supposed to grow older, but not have the aches and pains associated with old age.

Many will die and never find His secret place. How do we get to his secret place? Communicating and communing with God are essentials. This is to say that you must spend much time with God while having indebt conversation with Him. The bible says that God's children hear His voice and recognize that it is His voice. Communicating with Him is another way of saying that you have got to spend much time in prayer. Most people think that prayer is getting down on your knees and saying some long drawn out ritualistic rhetoric about deliverance from one's own problems or upheavals.

No, prayer is conversing with Jehovah-you talking to Him, and then listening to Him talk to you. So often times we simply talk to Him, and not ever wait and listen to what He has to say to us.

Communication with the creator is a direct way to tap into His omnipotent power.

On the bus, in the car, standing on the corner, or in the midst of a crowd, you can always talk to God and enter into His secret place.

When you are in His secret place, it doesn't matter what people say about you, or how they act towards you. His secret place puts a hedge around you that none can penetrate.

When we find God's secret place, we will find that our lives is not dependent upon who's on our side, or yet, who's our enemies. It won't matter, for we shall be a well of infinite power within ourselves.

The Apostle Paul was talking about the benefits of being in God's secret place when he penned Philippians 4:13. Note what he says:

13. I can do all things through Christ which strengthens me.

When we enter into communion and fellowship with God (His secret place), there is no limit to the power that we possess. Failure is not optional.

Too, observe what Paul says in Philippians 4:19:

19. But my God shall supply all your need according to his riches in glory by Christ Jesus.

This is why you entering into His secret place is so pivotal in your life-because all of your need shall be supplied. While occupying this mortal flesh, you shall have a degree of need-no matter how spiritual you shall become. You shall have some needs to be met.

You see, when I learn to commune with Him and spend quality time talking and listening to Him, I ease more into His secret place of power where he supplies all of my needs.

Jesus was alluding to the benefits of residing in His secret place when He taught His disciples in Matthew 6: 31-34:

31. Therefore take no thought, saying, what shall we eat? Or, what shall we drink? Or, wherewith shall we be clothed?
32. (For after all these things do the Gentiles seek) For your heavenly Father knows that you have need of all these things.
33. But seek you first the Kingdom of God, and his righteousness; and all these things shall be added unto you.

34. Take therefore no thought for tomorrow: for tomorrow shall take thought for the things of itself. Sufficient unto the day is the evil thereof.

Jesus is saying that when you learn to spend time with God, and learn to talk to Him and listen to Him, you won't have to concern yourself with whether or not you are going to be taken care of.

There are two main things that Jesus says in these verses: 1.God will take care of you, and 2. don't worry about tomorrow.

Another thing, that ushers you swiftly into His secret place, is **PRAISE.** Praise is the outward showing of adoration and affection to your God. It is displaying openly your spirit of thanksgiving. God notices and honors your praise. Nothing gets God's attention faster than your outward praise.

Our praise gets us into that inner chamber where God's power resides; it enables us to tap into it for whatever purpose that we should have.

In the book of Exodus, the 15th chapter, Moses and the people sang praises unto God for having brought them through the Red sea and drowned all of their enemies. They praised Him because it put them in His presence-in His secret place. Observe their song: Exodus 15: 1-3:

1. Then sang Moses and the children of Israel this song unto the Lord, and spoke, saying, I will sing unto the Lord, for he has triumphed gloriously: the horse and his rider has he thrown into the sea.
2. The Lord is my strength and song, and he is become my salvation: he is my God, and I will prepare him an habitation; my father's God, and I will exalt him.
3. The Lord is a man of war: the Lord is his name.

Their song was their praise to God. They knew that this wasn't the last enemy that they would face, and they knew that they needed to tap into God's power, and how did they do that? They tapped into supernatural power through their praise.

You see, you cannot buy or bride God, because He owns everything. Note Psalm 24: 1:

1. The earth is the Lord's, and the fullness thereof; the world, and they that dwell therein.

The Psalmist was simply saying that the earth and everything, and everybody on it is subject to the Lord-they have to give account to Him because He owns them. So, our praise gets him to afford us a degree of His power over them. In essence, He gives us the right to act as though our enemies belong to us, and we can dispose of them as we choose.

Note what King David says about praising the Lord in the 145 Palms, 1-6:

1. I will extol you, my God, O King; and I will bless your name forever and ever.
2. Every day ill I bless you; and I will praise your name forever and ever.
3. Great is the Lord, and greatly to be praised; and his greatness is unsearchable.
4. One generation shall praise your works to another, and shall declare your mighty acts.
5. I will speak of the glorious honor of majesty, and of your wondrous works
6. And men shall speak of the might of your terrible acts: and I will declare your greatness, and shall sing of your righteousness.

Never underestimate the power of your praise, for it will supply your needs, conquer your enemies, and lift you higher than you have ever been, because your praise puts you directly into the presence of God, and when you are in His presence, you can ask whatever you will, and it shall be done unto you.

Look at what God said to King David when he was in the presence of God. 2 Samuel 12: 7-8:

7. And Nathan said to David, You are the man. Thus says the Lord God of Israel, I anointed you king over Israel, and I delivered you out of the hand of Saul;

8. And I gave you your master's house, and your master's wives into your bosom, and gave you're the house of Israel and of Judah; and if that had been too little, I would moreover have given unto you such and such things.

Note, God tells David, "If that had not been enough, I would have given you such and such things."

God was telling King David that when he was in His presence, all he had to do was ask for whatever he wanted.

Praise Him, and it will put you into the presence of God, and there, you will find unlimited favor from God.

CHAPTER EIGHT

DISCIPLE, NURTURE, DEVELOP, MATURE

We are the light; sanctified children of the light-sanctified simply mean to be set aside. God resides in His children.

The whole of mankind is dependent upon the birth and knowledge "of self" in the children of Jehovah. We determine the status of the world, even in our ignorance. Observe what Jehovah says in the book of 2 Chronicles 7: 12-14:

12. And the Lord appeared to Solomon by night, and said unto him, I have heard your prayer, and have chosen this place to myself for an house of sacrifice.
13. If I shut up heaven that there be no rain, or if I command the locusts to devour the land, or if I send pestilence among my people;
14. If my people, which are called by my name, shall humble themselves, and pray, and seek my face, and turn from their wicked ways; then will I hear from heaven, and will forgive their sin, and will heal their land.

God says that if His people, those that serve Him, would do something as they are supposed to do-walk in humility, pray, seek Him, turn from their wicked ways, then, He would heal the land. The children of God have to know their place and stand in it, then, the world would be delivered. The Children of God simply failing to walk in the fullness of who they are disrupts all of mankind-even nature itself. We were the ones chosen to set the captives free.

We have the power dormant within us to change every circumstance, any condition, and set straight all the crooked. God has already placed the power in us.

We must be trained and taught how to engage and tap into that for which we already have resting in our bosom. We are the Sons of The Most High God-Jehovah. Note what He says in the book of Jeremiah 31: 33:

33. But this shall be the covenant that I will make with the house of Israel; after those days, says the Lord, I will put my law in their inward parts, and write it in their hearts; and will be their God, and they shall be my people.

God is telling the prophet Jeremiah that He and His covenant law will be on the inside of those that believes on Him. In other words, His power shoots from the inside of us; that is why the Psalmist says that we are Gods- because God resides in us, and we have opportunity and privilege to His awesome power.

There are four distinct ways to come into the fullness of who you really are in Jehovah and the world. They are:

1. Disciple
2. Nurture
3. Develop
4. Mature

Failure to grasp these four stages, will handicap you as a believer. Let us observe them individually:

1. **Disciple** simply means one that accepts and assists in spreading the doctrine of another in hopes of making new disciples. If you believe in God, some disciple converted you, thereby making you a disciple. Now you must go and make other disciples. We cannot be an island off to ourselves. We must attempt to convert others to the doctrines of God. They world does not just naturally know God Jehovah. We must convert them into disciples.

I was asked a few days ago what was my mission for the church that I pastor. I told them my mission is the same as it was given by Jehovah to Jesus and Jesus to us-Go make new disciples. So often churches get lost in celebrating annual days-Men day, women day, choir day, church anniversary, pastor anniversary etc....etc.....etc. They neglect their mission.

The main thrust of the church, the believer, is to **MAKE NEW DISCIPLES!** Everything else is built around and supports this premise. The primary definition of a church is a collection of believers thriving to make new disciples.

If we fail to make new disciples, the world becomes a mass of ignorance in Godliness and spirituality, and thus, live lives of despair and defeat; never fully understanding who they really are.

2. **Nurture** simply means to care for in such a way that it produces growth. Nurturing the new disciple is paramount, for it is in this stage that they learn "how to be and become" the royal seed of Jehovah. More often than not, we get caught up in entertaining them, and just making the new disciple become accustomed to "feeling good", but not growing spiritually-thereby, living quiet lives of defeat. In essence, shouting on Sunday, but beaten financially, physically, emotionally, psychologically, and spiritually. They only have a form of godliness. Note what the Apostle Paul says of this matter in 2 Timothy 3: 1-5: 1. This know also, that in the last days perilous times shall come. 2. For men shall be lovers of their on selves, covetous, boasters, proud, blasphemers, disobedient to parents, unthankful, unholy, 3. Without natural affection, trucebreakers, false accusers, incontinent, fierce, despisers of those that are good, 4. Traitors, heady, high-minded, lovers of pleasures more than lovers of God; 5. Having a form of godliness but denying the power thereof: from such turn away. We must nurture the disciples, for it is the quintessential of being a true disciple. Nurturing is how we learn to break the yokes that have bound us for so long. Paul says that it is not enough to have a form of godliness; we must walk in the newness of who we really are, and this, inevitably, can only happen through nurturing. Exactly how do we nurture? Through teaching godly principals, in depth bible study, collective prayer, and hands on guidance. We must be accountable for someone and to someone. You cannot grow yourself. Someone has to sow into your life-particularly the new disciple. Observe what the Psalmist says in the book of Psalms 27: 17: Iron sharpens iron; so a man sharpens the countenance of his friend. The disciple must avail themselves to someone that will help them grow into the fullness of what Jehovah has called them to. You cannot skip nurturing and become the saint that you were designed to be.

3. **Develop**. Develop means to grow and become. What most do not realize is that godliness is a growing process. No, when one is first disciple, one is nowhere near what they shall be and become. If you were a heavy user of profanity when you first became a disciple, that profane tongue didn't just leave you. No, you had to learn how to control that profane tongue, and over the years, you learned to control it. If you were a whoremonger, that desire for promiscuous sex does not just up and leave and never comes back; no, sometimes, even while you are following after Jehovah, your flesh will desire to be whorish sometimes, but through development, you learn how to take control of your weakened, but strengthening flesh. Develop means to continue to become better and stronger; to gradually ascend to a higher level in **Jehovah**.

Lack of development is the reason some believers remain the same year after year. They struggle with the same problems over and over again. You see, the devil will not use any new ploys if the ones that he has used over and over again on you still work. When you develop, you are migrating higher and higher. A sign that you are developing is when the things that use to bother you don't bother you any more-or, at least, not as much. You will always handle cataclysms-personal or otherwise, miserably if you fail to continue to develop. My prayer life must develop; my work life must develop, and my thought life must develop. Note what Paul says on the importance of developing. Ephesians 4: 22-24: 22. That you put off concerning the former conversation the old man, which is corrupt according to the deceitful lusts; 23. And be renewed in the spirit of your mind; 24. And that you put on the new man, which after God is created in righteousness and true holiness. Paul is stressing your development as a disciple of Jehovah. He says for us to "Put on", which means for us to choose to develop in our minds and our character as a disciple; for if you fail to develop, then your life will cancel out what you are saying. People are more apt to believe when they see what you do, rather than just hearing what you are saying. Mere words are empty without accompanying deeds. In developing, I experience great degrees of pain, and learn to control the way that I respond to its discomfort, for Pain from friends and foe helps me to grow and become. I am developing; I am developing, and I shall continue to develop until I depart this mortal flesh of mine given me by my creator. You must develop and develop until you become the image of Him. This is what the bible was alluding to in Ephesian 4: 11-13: 11. And he gave some, apostles; and some, prophets; and some, evangelists; and some, pastors and teachers; 12. For the perfecting of the saints, for the work of the ministry, for the edifying of the body of Christ: 13. Until we all come in the unity of the faith, and of the knowledge of the Son of God, unto a perfect man, unto the measure of the stature of the fullness of Christ. Our development is designed to mold us into the likeness of Jehovah through Christ. Most undeveloped, or shall I say under-developed believers think that we are supposed to worship Jesus, but Jesus wanted us to focus on the Father-Jehovah. Observe what Jesus said in the book of John concerning this matter: John 16: 23-25: 23. And in that day you shall ask me nothing. Verily, verily, I say unto you, Whatsoever you shall ask the Father in my name, he will give it you. 24. Heretofore have you asked nothing in my name: ask, and you shall receive, that your joy may be full. 25. These things have I spoken unto you in proverbs: but the time comes, when I shall no more speak unto you in proverbs, but I shall show you plainly of the Father. Jesus is saying that His desire and purpose is to teach us to look to Jehovah; to worship Jehovah, and to praise Jehovah; that is why development is so pertinent to us as believers. We must grow and develop to know that we don't need a middle man to talk to the Father for us-like the High Priest did in the Old Testament. No, we develop to where we go to Jehovah's thrown for ourselves and others who has not fully developed as we have. When we develop, we become a vessel that Jehovah can use to His glory.

4. **Mature**. Mature means that development is complete. You are a disciple; you have been nurtured, and because you were nurtured, you developed. Now you enter into maturity. The reason why some churches (believers) argue and fuss and fight all the time is because they have not been nurtured, and because they have not been nurtured, they have not developed, and because they have not developed, they have not matured. Again, development is a process; it just does not happen overnight. Too, development will not just serendipitously happen; you will not accidently develop. No, one must desire to develop, and, in order to do that, you must not allow yourself to be satisfied with where you are. You must adamantly press yourself to develop, and connect yourself to those who have developed to where you want to be. Note what the Apostle Paul says on the matter of developing. Galatians 3: 13-14: Brothers, I count not myself to have apprehended: but this one thing I do, forgetting those things which are behind, and reaching forth unto those things which are before, 14. I press toward the mark for the prize of the high calling of God in Christ Jesus. In essence, Paul is saying that he is still being developed; and when he says that he is pressing, he is stressing that development can sometimes be very difficult, so one has to be determined to develop and grow.

Mature basically means to have developed and reached a designed desired state.

Maturity is reaching the status to be "Christ like". You see, maturity affords us that ambidextrous kind of faith-where, on the one hand, we thank Jehovah for His many blessings that He has so graciously given unto us, and at the same time, we also appreciate the hard times and hardships we so often encounter.

We matured enough to thank Him for both, for one brings us joy, and the other forces us to discern that God does what's best for us.

Maturity helps us to understand that there is purpose in our pain. Observe how the Psalmist notes ambidextrous faith; Psalms 30: 3-5:

3. O Lord, you have brought up my soul from the grave: you have kept me alive, that I should not go down to the pit.
4. Sing unto the Lord, O you saints of his, and give thanks at the remembrance of his holiness.
5. For his anger endures but a moment; in his favor is life: weeping may endure for a night, but joy comes in the morning.

What King David is saying is you might have some degree of sorrow, but at the same time, you shall have some joy. Ambidextrous means a person has the ability to use both hands just as well; instead of being just right handed or left handed. When you have grown, developed, and matured, you can handle having joy in one hand and sorrow in the other; praise in one hand, and hardship in the other; laughter in one hand, and tears in the other.

When you have reached maturity, you still praise Him in-spite of what you are going through because you know that all things work together for your good.

When I was developing, I experienced the discomfort of pain, and I didn't like it, so I tried to avoid pain at all cost. But, when I matured, I understand that there is purpose to my pain, and that pain often produces growth; yes, there is no growth without pain, but you cannot understand and appreciate that until you become matured in Jehovah.

I learned and accepted that growth, pain, and loss all work together to propel me to my destiny.

Remember, just coming to church and faithfully being in the building will not develop and mature you; no, you have got to want to grow spiritually. Growing spiritually will help you deal with the pain and discomfort of life.

CHAPTER NINE

GOD'S PATIENCE

P atience, as defined by the dictionary, is the capacity to accept and tolerate delay, trouble, or suffering without getting angry or upset-an ability or willingness to suppress restlessness or annoyance when confronted with delay.

In a nut shell, or in laymen terms, it is acquiring or learning how to face and accept your daily troubles and setbacks without falling apart and getting angry. Patience, is experiencing the delay, even if it is not your fault and beyond your control, with calmness and displaying a cool disposition. Now, we understand why it is said that patience is a virtue.

But, true patience, is a gift from Jehovah; for it is most difficult for one to learn to be patient in an impatient world. No, it is given by God-thus, is the reason why we refer to it as "God's Patience", for it is truly inhuman to endure delay of rescue, troubles, storms, hardships, sickness, lost and whatever disturbing situation one might encounter, and not become unraveled or upset.

It is very difficult to be patient, but even more difficult to remain patient for any length of time.

There is no man in the bible that defines being patient more than Job. When speaking of patience, most men allude to the righteous man in the bible called Job. Eight verses in the first chapter of the book of Job describe patience completely. Note: chapter 1: 14-22:

14. And there came a messenger unto Job, and said, The oxen were plowing, and the asses feeding, beside them:
15. And the Sabeans fell upon them, and took them away; yea, they have slain the servants with the edge of the sword; and I only am escaped alone to tell you.
16. While he was yet speaking, there came also another, and said, The fire of God is fallen from heaven, and has burned up the sheep, and the servants, and consumed them; and I only am escaped alone to tell you.
17. While he was yet speaking, there came also another, and said, The Chaldeans made out three bands, and fell upon the camels, and have carried them away, yes, and slain the servants with the edge of the sword; and I only am escaped alone to tell you.

18. While he was yet speaking, there came also another, and said, Your sons and your daughters were eating and drinking wine in their eldest brother's house:

19. And, behold, there came a great wind from the wilderness, and smote the four corners of the house, and it fell upon the young men, and they are dead; and I only am escaped alone to tell you.

20. Then Job arose, and rent his mantle, and shaved his head, and fell down upon the ground, and worshipped;

21. And said, Naked came I out of my mother's womb, and naked shall I return there: the Lord gave, and the Lord has taken away; blessed be the name of the Lord.

22. In all this Job sinned not, nor charged God foolishly.

Because of all that Job went through in just a short period of time, he is referred to as the most patient man that has ever lived.

And, while most folks do not know this or fail to mention it, Job's patience soon ran out, and Jehovah has to chasten him.

Few realize and know that Job's patience ran out. In Job chapter 38-41, Jehovah sternly verbally chastens Job.

This is a testament that it is impossible to remain patience without God, for human patients will soon run out.

Patience is how we continue to possess the ability to walk in The Light of God. Walking in the light will give us godly patience. True patience comes from Jehovah.

In order to walk in His perfect will and plan for us, we must acquire His patience, for He does not always operate on our time or during our season. We must have the patience to wait. Note what the prophet Isaiah says about God: Isaiah 55: 8-9:

8. For my thoughts are not your thoughts, neither are your ways my ways, says the Lord.

9. For as the heavens are higher than the earth, so are my ways higher than your ways, and my thoughts than your thoughts.

God doesn't think like man, nor does He act like man, therefore, He doesn't respond like a man does; hence, we must learn godly patience to walk in the light of God's secret place where we can acquire His strength, power, and fortitude to walking in the fullness of His love and power where we can fulfill our holy destiny and calling.

It is imperative for us to learn to wait on Him if we are to continue to walk in the Light. As alluded to before. Note the benefits of walking in the light and patiently waiting on Jehovah: Isaiah 40: 29-30:

29. He gives power to the faint; and to them that have no might he increases strength.
30. Even the youths shall faint and be weary, and the young men shall utterly fall:
31. But they that wait upon the Lord shall renew their strength; they shall mount up with wings as eagles; they shall run, and not be weary; and they shall walk, and not faint.

Now, it becomes apparent why it is said that patience is a virtue.

We mustn't try to put God on our time schedule, but we must get in His time frame and wait upon Him with patience, and watch the Light watch the Light evolve around us and shoot forth from us that others might see the power of The Almighty resting upon us.

Wait on the Lord: be of good courage, and he shall strengthen your heart: wait, I say, on the Lord. Psalm 27: 14.

CHAPTER TEN

PROTECTED BY THE LIGHT

When you dwell in God's secret place, you are protected by the light, which is the spirit and essence of The Most High. Satan cannot touch you unless given prior permission by God. Note Job 1: 8-10:

8. And the Lord said unto Satan, Have you considered my servant Job, that there is none like him in the earth, a perfect and an upright man, one that fears God, and eschews evil?
9. Then Satan answered the Lord, and said, Does Job fear God for nothing?
10. Has not you made an hedge about him, and about his house, and about all that he has on every side? You have blessed the work of his hands, and his substance is increased in the land.

You see, what the text is saying essentially is that God has a protective hedge around all who serves Him. No harm can come to you unless He first gives them permission to do so, and if He does give them permission, it is still for your good.

Note what the Apostle Paul says of things working for you; Romans 8: 28:

And we know that all things works together for good to them that love God, to them who are the called according to his purpose.

In other words, whatever befalls you, God causes it to work for your betterment. Hence, you will always fall forward.

The light of God is like the physical property of light. As long as the light shines, darkness of any kind is dispelled. It remains out of the presence and reaches of the light.

When you enter God's secret place, His light, His presence, it automatically pushes away the darkness of the evil enemy. Where we err at is when we step out of the light, and try to operate on our own; that why just being very religious is not enough. The enemy of light does not care how deeply religious you-it concerns itself with how much light you possess.

When we are in the light of God, we possess all the powers of God; His glory overshadows us. We have whatever power that God has; we become, in fact, God's glory in the flesh.

The Apostle Paul was alluding to who we are and what we possess when he discussed this principal referring to us as heirs and co-hears of Christ-heirs of The Father, and co-heirs with the son; that is why the bible is referred to as the Old Testament and the New Testament. Testament means that something and some things were left to us.

Thus, is the reason why Christ had to die first. The Will is no good unless the testator dies. Note scripture: Hebrews 9: 16-17

16. For where a testament is, there must also of necessity be the death of the testator.
17. For a testament is of force after men are dead: otherwise it is of no strength at all while the testator lives.

The Will puts us in the Light, in God's secret place; the place of power. The Will equips us to do battle with the powers of darkness.

One of our greatest adversaries is ignorance. You see, the most unfortunate thing about us is that we can be saved, holy spirit filled, fire baptized, and go to heaven when we die, but if we do not consciously walk in the Light and power of God, we can live daily quiet lives of defeat; that's why Paul says that the entire creation is dependent upon us-it waits for The Children of light to awaken to their true "God Self".

Observe: Romans 8: 19-22:

19. For the earnest expectation of the creature waits for the manifestation of the sons of God.
20. For the creature was made subject to vanity, not willingly, but by reason of him who has subjected the same in hope.
21. Because the creature itself also shall be delivered from the bondage of corruption into the glorious liberty of the children of God.
22. For e know that the whole creation groans and travails in pain together until now.

The whole creation waits in pain for the children of Light to realize their true selves, and walk in the glory and power of God the Father.

The Light puts a holy supernatural hedge around us so that the powers of darkness cannot prevail against us. We have that holy power by virtue of who we are. The disciples gave us a glimpse of this supernatural power in the book of Luke when they came back from mission and was reporting their acts to Jesus. Note Luke 10: 17:

And the seventy returned again with joy, saying, Lord, even the devils are subject unto us through your name.

They were saying that the devils of the "other world" are subject to them-the devils have to obey them!

Note what Jesus says to them in that 19th verse:

Behold, I give unto you power to tread on serpents and scorpions, and over all the power of the enemy: and nothing shall by any means hurt you.

Thus, you have power, and you are protected by the Supreme Holy God!

Now, you should understand why the devil wants you to just be religious, and be into things and stuff-anything to get you to not realize and live in your true and real identity. The devil knows that your potential is unlimited; there is nothing that you cannot do or accomplish as long as you walk in the light-Jehovah's secret place.

God has commissioned us to deliver the whole of man from the fall of man-perpetrated upon us through the first man- Adam.

Oftentimes it saddens me to hear preachers and lay people tell the masses that material things are indications of God's presence; while this can be true, it is often not the case. Many try to prove to others materialistically that they are in God's favor, so they go out and try to get as much stuff as they can to imply the presence of Jehovah in their lives; but, just having things, does not automatically mean that it is God that is blessing you. Sometimes the devil will give you things to make you deviate from your calling and purpose. Look what he offered Jesus: Matthew 4: 8-9:

8. Again, the devil takes him up into an exceedingly high mountain. And shows him all the kingdoms of the world, and the glory of them;

9. And says unto him, All these things ill I give you, if you will fall down and worship me.

The devil tells Jesus that he would give him all "these things" if He would just fall down on His knees and worship him. He tried to temp the humanistic side of Jesus.

The devil knows that stuff, so often, drive us away from Jehovah because we put a lot of effort and time into keeping and protecting our "stuff"-to the point to whereby we neglect our relationship and fellowship with God.

Walk in the Light, and the material things, all that you need and more, will come to you.

Remember, the more that you focus on the Word of God, live by it, digest it, and let it guild your life, the more that you will affect the presence of God. Meditate upon God, while doing so, have an active prayer life (daily talking to Jehovah); when you do these things, you will walk in the Light of God, and thereby, dwell in God's secret place.

CHAPTER ELEVEN

STEPPING OUT OF DARKNESS

What most of us do not know and realize is that when God created us, we were not supposed to ever get sick, or have lack and need, and we were never supposed to die because we were created to live in the light and presence of Jehovah forever, but Adam sinned, and alienated man from the eternal presence of God.

No, we were never to experience cancer, heart disease, or any other kind of sickness and disease. And, we were supposed to live eternally- never die physically! Note what Jehovah says to Adam about life and death. Genesis 2: 17:

> 17. But of the tree of the knowledge of good and evil, you shall not eat of it: for in the day that you eat thereof you shall surely die.

Thus, God says to Adam, "If you eat this, you'll die." We can safely conclude that if Adam didn't eat from the tree of knowledge, he would never have experienced death; for if he was already supposed to die, then God would not have said "when" you eat you'll die.

From these early texts in Genesis, we can also see that the devil's desire is to kill man; for he leads man to eat from the tree of knowledge, but purposely fails to lead man to eat from the tree of life. Why, because he wanted man to die.

Man could have eaten from the tree of life and lived forever and also known good and evil because he had already eaten from the tree of knowledge. Note Genesis 3: 22:

> 22. And the Lord God said, Behold, the man is become as one of us, to know good and evil: and now, less he put forth his hand, and take also of the tree of life, and eat and live forever.

The devil didn't entice him to eat from the tree of life because he wanted the man to die.

You must choose to live; choose to come out of darkness into light- choose to live while you are living, and refuse to die until you die.

Because of Adam, we can't get pass dying. Note: Hebrews 9: 27:

27. And as it is appointed unto men once to die, but after this the judgment.

Appointed death means that it has been assigned for you to die someday, but, observe that the text says "but" after this the judgment. Now, of course, the word "but" is a conjunction, which means that it is connected to what has just been said. It is a contrast word-this means that what he is about to say after the "but" contrasts to what he has just said. He says, "But judgment"; which means that judgment has the possibility to alter your death sentence. Look at the book of Revelation 20: 12-15:

12. And I saw the dead, small and great, stand before God; and the books were opened, and another book was opened, which is the book of life: and the dead were judged out of those things which were written in the books, according to their works.
13. And the sea gave up the dead which were in it; and death and hell delivered up the dead which were in them: and they were judged every man according to their works.
14. And death and hell were cast into the lake of fire. This is the second death.
15. And whosoever was not found written in the book of life was cast into the lake of fire.

In other words, we shall die someday, but we don't have to remain dead, or experience the second death.

But, while in this life, we can choose to truly live while we are living. Speak to the king in you-the royal seed of God, and experience the power and nature of God work through you.

Note what the Apostle Peter says about us walking in the light of God. 1 Peter 2: 9:

9. But you are a chosen generation, a peculiar people; that you should show forth the praises of him who has called you out of darkness into his marvelous light.

The word peculiar means something that is abnormal, and the word marvelous means something that is supernatural, amazing, and awesome.

Now here is what Peter is saying, God has chosen His people to be abnormal in this world, to show His supernatural, awesome, and amazing blessings that He showers down upon His people.

Abnormal means going against being normal; to not be one of the regular status of man's "normal".

Generation is a specific group of people that are different; people that have chosen to be abnormal and amazingly supernatural. They show God's blessing in their lives. They demonstrate the benefits of walking in the light of God.

Because of Adam's sin, it is normal for man to live and walk in darkness. He lives outside of the purpose and will of God-his creator. Sin started with Adam's disobedience in eating from the tree of knowledge of good and evil. Every man that followed Adam, "naturally" walked in the footsteps of his father, Adam; without trying, he walks in darkness because that is all that he naturally knows.

Darkness is anything outside of the will of God; too, it means "unknown", not being able to discern-without light, therefore, without sight, or insight.

From his birth to his grave, man learns to live in darkness, to such a depth until he cannot appreciate anything outside of his inherit darkness.

Man expects to be sick; he expects a trouble filled life; he expects to be broke and live in need; he expects to be in debt; he expects to live in despair with a life filled with curses of which he himself cannot break; and, the disheartening thing about it all is man teaches his children this darkened defeated life outside of God.

To them, God becomes this far away being in some heavenly place beyond the stars, and they sooth themselves with religion by going to church to only have glimpses of a God of which they know not, or know very little of.

Their satisfaction from attending church is to fulfill their obligation of having attended church; thus is the reason why many lives are not changed, and defeat runs in their ranks rampantly.

Thus, he is until someone discovers **The Light of God** and moves into His **Secret Place**, and then leads someone else to the light.

Hence, we get the definition of "mission"-to teach others how to come to the light and how to live in the light and dwell in God's secret place.

Jesus was telling His disciples to teach others how to come and walk in the light. Observe: Matthew 28: 18-20:

18. And Jesus came and spoke unto them, saying, All power is given unto me in Heaven and in earth.
19. Go you therefore, and teach all nations, baptizing them in the name of the Father, and of the Son, and of the Holy Ghost.
20. Teaching them to observe all things whatsoever I have commanded you: and, lo, I am with you always, even unto the end of the world. A-men.

Jesus was telling them to go everywhere and teach men how to come out of darkness; and he says to them not to go in their own power but in His power that was given unto Him by His father Jehovah.

This is what Peter was alluding to when he says that God called us out of darkness into the marvelous light. Remember, peculiar means abnormal, and marvelous means extraordinary and supernatural.

The light of God is amazing, extraordinary, and supernatural; hence, if we walk in the light of God, we become extraordinary and supernatural people that men will be amazed by.

As created beings, formed from the dust of the ground, we are "natural" beings. We are limited by our natural bodies. In our own might, we can only do natural things. We cannot get passed our "natural" selves; for God's law demand that if we are to experience the natural world, then we must inhabit a natural body; that is why the devil tries to possess a man's body-so that he can experience natural things. He cannot get pass God's divine law pertaining to His created earth.

Jehovah is a spiritual super God that dwells and rides upon the air, the clouds, the stars, and the earth-thus, He dwells above men, beyond men, amongst men.

When we are in the light of God, He takes part of His super self, and bath (anoint) our natural self with it. We become supernatural beings reeling the power of The Almighty God.

We must intently desire the light of God, for then and only then will we truly find His secret place. God's secret place is when God puts you in His light. It is called "secret place" because it is in a state that the devil and no one else can figure out how to get to you to harm you. Your enemies and the devil see you, but they can't touch you because you are protected by the power and might of the Almighty God. It is like you are on display, and God is daring the devil and anyone else to try and touch you.

CHAPTER TWELVE

LET TRUTH BE YOUR GUIDE

If truth be truly revealed of "who" the children of God are, one would find that they are an esoteric group called out by God to walk in His holy omnipotent power upon the earth-while yet inhabiting a carnal body.

As human beings, we are designed by Jehovah with three parts to our being-a body, a soul, and a spirit. God ascribe to the esoteric group that He empowered to live in the spirit even while enclosed by flesh.

That is the only way that, we as believers, can fully exhibit Jehovah's grace and power upon human kind.

The truth then, is anything that God has done or said!

Look how the Apostle Paul explains it when referring to the Believers walking in the Truth. Ephesians 2: 10:

10. For we are His workmanship, created in Christ Jesus unto good works, which God has before ordained that we should walk in them.

Note Ephesians 5: 14:

14. Wherefore he says, Awake you that sleeps, and arise from the dead, and Christ shall give you light.

In other words, Paul is saying that you have got to be sleep and dead not to walk in the light of the power that Jehovah has given you; that is why he says, "Wake up! Dead man." Possess, right now, what is yours.

Again observe what the Apostle Paul says to the esoteric few that has been chosen to walk in the light of the Truth; Galatians 5: 16:

16. This I say then, Walk in the spirit, and you shall not fulfill the lust of the flesh.

Our carnal bodies resist our spiritual selves-it craves natural things of the world, and denies the spirit side of us.

No, you will not just serendipitously walk in the truth of the light. You have got to purposely, intentionally, find the truth and live in it.

Design your daily life in the truth, and then you shall see miracles and wonders of the Father of all creation.

If He stresses to us to walk in truth, then there has to, innately, be a propensity for us to "live" a lie; for a lie is the direct opposite of the truth. Truth is illuminated because there is a lie. What is the lie- That we are wholly and only flesh, plagued by the physicality's of mere human existence.

As previously stated, the lie is that we are supposed to be sick, diseased, broke, defeated, weak, and without supernatural powers.

But now look at the truth, Deuteronomy 28: 1-13:

1. And it shall come to pass, if you shall hearken diligently unto the voice of the Lord your God, to observe and to do all his commandments which I command you this day, that the Lord your God will set you on high above all nations of the earth:
2. And all these blessings shall come on you, and overtake you, if you shall hearken unto the voice of the Lord your God.
3. Blessed shall you be in the city, and blessed shall you be in the field.
4. Blessed shall be the fruit of your body, and the fruit of your ground, and the fruit of your cattle, the increase of your kine, and the flocks of your sheep.
5. Bless shall be your basket and your store.
6. Bless shall you be when you come in, and blessed shall you be when you go out.
7. The Lord shall cause your enemies that rise up against you to be smitten before your face: they shall come out against you one way, and flee before you seven ways.
8. The Lord shall command the blessing upon you in your storehouses, and in all that you set your hand unto; and he shall bless you in the land which the Lord your God gives you.
9. The Lord shall establish you an holy people unto himself, as he has sworn unto you, if you shall keep the commandments of the Lord your God, and walk in his ways.
10. And all people of the earth shall see that you are called by the name of the Lord; and they shall be afraid of you.

11. And the Lord shall make you plenteous in goods, in the fruit of your body, and in the fruit of your cattle, and in the fruit of your ground, in the land which the Lord swore unto your fathers to give you.

12. The Lord shall open unto you his good treasure, the heaven to give the rain unto your land in his season, and to bless all the work of your hand; and you shall lend unto many nations, and you shall not borrow.

13. And the Lord shall make you the head, and not the tail; and you shall be above only, and you shall not be beneath; if that you hearken unto the commandments of the Lord your God, which I command you this day, to observe and to do them:

The truth, as Moses so eloquently put it, is that we are the blessed of the Lord-His magnificent workmanship that He personally crafted to be just like Him- Children of the Most High God encapsulated by flesh.

As children of the most High Jehovah, we are the light bearers. We expose the real truth.

The reason why we are called light bearers is because we unveil, or expose the truth. We are supposed to guild men to the truth (the instructions of Jehovah for men's lives).

When we examine Moses exposition in Deuteronomy chapter 28, we find that we are supernaturally blessed. Blessed literally means to be holy and consecrated; that is the dictionary's literal meaning of the word blessed, but to put it in laymen's term though, blessed means to enjoy the bliss of heaven while on earth.

We cannot allow ourselves to be offset by the contrary things that might happen in our lives; for whatever happens in our lives is designed by Jehovah for our good. Romans 8:28:

28. And we know that all things work together for good to them that love God, to them who are the called according to his purpose.

That's God's truth; so then, that means that whatever contrary or otherwise that I am going through, I can get through it because it has already been designed for my good. So, if I fall, I fall forward; it helps me to rise.

All are God's truth for you. The only way that these principles are stopped or offset, is when you stop believing and refuse to acknowledge and believe the truth-what God has said about you!

You have got to purpose with all of your heart to walk in God's truth for your life-what He has purposed for you.

You cannot trust yourself-what you see or do not see; because your flesh will deceive you. Note what the Apostle Paul says about your flesh. Romans 7:14-23:

14. For we know that the law is spiritual: but I am carnal, sold under sin.
15. For that which I do I allow not: for what I would, that do I not; but what I hate, that do I.
16. If then I do that which I would not, I consent unto the law that it is good.
17. Now then it is no more I that do it, but sin that dwells in me.
18. For I know that is in,e (that is, in my flesh,) dwells no good thing: for to will is present with me, but how to perform that which is good I find not.
19. For the good that I would I do not: but the evil which I would not, that I do.
20. Now if I do that I would not, it is no more I that do it, but sin that dwells in me.
21. I find then a law, that, when I would do good, evil is present with me.
22. For I delight in the law of God after the inward man:
23. But I see another law in my members, warring against the law If my mind, and bringing me into captivity to the law of sin which is in my members.

This means that I have got to go against my natural body and the natural belief that has been instilled in me, perhaps all of my life; and believe what God says about me and for me.

The Apostle Paul is saying that your flesh do not want to operate in the spiritual realm, or in the supernatural. Your natural self, despise the light; it prefers the darkness of the lie; it fights and wants to believe what it has been taught. It naturally wants to follow the lead of other carnal beings and be bound by natural things; that are not God's design for your life; that is not the truth-the light.

His truth is supernatural! To walk in His truth, is to walk in the supernatural; to expect the supernatural, thus, to perform supernatural feats; that is why it is called "the light" remember-it uncovers and unveils your real true self in God.

Truth is, you are a god! I know that that thought blows most men away because man refuse to see himself as he was created to be-just like his Father God-Jehovah. That is scripture: Observe Psalms 82:6:

> 6. I have said, You are gods; and all of your are children of the most high.

> ...

What the Palmist is saying is that we are gods because we were created by the Most High God, therefore, we are His children; thus, we are, in fact, gods encapsulated by flesh (I continue to stress this in hope that you will get it).

In the natural, this carnal flesh, we start to die from the first minute that we enter into this world; we die a little bit every day until we go to the grave, but the spirit part of us lives on and on and on.

Death and dying within the ranks of the living is a part of the curse of Adam. We cannot stop the curse, but we can have victory on earth while we head towards the grave. It is our choice. Look what the Apostle John says: John 1:1/ 12:

> 1. In the beginning was the Word, and the Word was with God, and the Word was God.
> 12. But as many as received him, to them gave he power to become the sons of God, even to them that believe on his name:

Note what John says, in essence, we can choose not to be bound in this carnal world. We must choose to walk in the light of Jehovah. John says that when we receive Him, He gives us the power "to become" sons of God.

It does not just happen. No, we have to choose to walk in the light and power of our heavenly Father while living on earth; which is to say that we should walk in the light while dwelling amongst darkness. We must let our lights shine in the midst of all of this darkness.

I choose to be healthy; I choose to be debt free; I choose to be a lender and not a borrower; I choose to be the head and not the tail; I choose to walk in the light and fullness of God my Father. I choose to make a difference among my brothers and sisters; I choose to be a guild to the blind and them that walk in darkness.

Lastly, observe John 1:14:

14. And the Word was made flesh, and dwelt among us, (and we beheld his glory, the glory as of the only begotten of the Father,) full of grace and truth.

In other words, the God-man, that we call Jesus is in fact and truth, the literal Word of God. Hence, God spoke some words, and when the words left his mouth, they formed and shaped and took on human form, which we now call Jesus.

Thus, just like our creator, our words become vehicles to accomplish whatever we desire it to…..Just like our heavenly Father.

We must walk in the Light; hide ourselves in the Light and guild others out of darkness.

And just like Jesus, we must show the world our glory which we ascertained from Jehovah-our Father. Now, the definition of the word glory means high renown or honor won by notable achievement; it means magnificent, great beauty; great honor and praise worthiness.

There is no glory to display if you are just like the people of darkness. Darkness cannot cast out darkness; only light can dispel darkness. When you unveil your glory, it makes the children of darkness desire to walk in the light that you walk in.

When you allow the glory, that God has placed upon you, to shine forth, it automatically chases the darkness that is filled with sickness, debt, want, death and disease away.

Walk in the light and watch those dark inhabited things vanish like the night during the early morning ushering in of a new day.

CHAPTER THIRTEEN

THE COMPANY THAT YOU KEEP

2 Corinthians 6:14-18:

14. Be you not unequally yoked together with unbelievers: for what fellowship has righteousness with unrighteousness? And what communion has light with darkness?
15. And what concord has Christ with Belial? Or what part has he that believes with and infidel?
16. And what agreement has the temple of God with idols? For you are the temple of the living God; as God has said, I will dwell in them, and walk in them; and I will be their God, and they shall be my people.
17. Wherefore come out from among them, and be you separate, says the Lord, and touch not the unclean thing; and I will receive you,
18. And will be a Father unto you, and you shall be my sons and daughters, says the Lord Almighty.

In order to walk in the light and power of God, you cannot keep company with those that walk in darkness-those that are contrary to you.

It is commonly thought in the world that opposites attract, but this is not so. Those things that are most alike are attracted to each other. This point is illustrated in how God set up marriage. Nothing destroys a marriage quicker than two people being unequally yoked together; that is why the bible says that God created a help meet for Adam. What that simply meant was twofold-someone that was right for him, and someone that would help and assist him.

God was demonstrating that not everyone was right for Adam, and Adam needed someone to assist and help him.

If in any marriage that you have, that the man doesn't provide and the woman fails to assist and help, their marriage will inevitably end. It will become overly burdensome and cumbersome for one or the other.

So it is in the spiritual realm. One cannot dwell with those that walk in darkness and refuse the light of God. You will never find God's secret place amidst darkness. He is the Light.

He says for His children of light to come out from among them and be separate; if not, you risk becoming darkened and losing The Light.

Observe what Joshua says to the children of Israel about the foreign nations-nations that operated in the darkness and knew not the Light of Jehovah. Joshua 23:5-6:

5. And the lord your God, he shall expel them from before you, and drive them from out of your sight; and you shall possess their land, as the lord your God has promised unto you.
6. Be you therefore very courageous to keep and to do all that is written in the book of the law of Moses, that you turn not aside There from to the right hand or to the left;

God told Joshua to tell the people to expel the inhabitants from the land that they had conquered.

The reason that God does this is plain and simple; He did not want those people that worshiped other Gods to influence His people.

You become just like those of which you fellowship with the most; either they shall change you, or you shall change them. Differences do not remain differences forever; one or the other will cross over to the other's side.

The company that you are keeping is either helping you walk in the light, or enticing you to walk away from the light into outer darkness. They are making you better or worst.

It is better for you to dwell by yourself than to dwell with bad company-walk alone than walk with someone that is not good for you.

One can tell a lot about a man by the company that he keeps. Those that you choose as friends speak volume of you.

As much as they might like each other, the lion and the lamb cannot dwell together; sooner or later, the lion will eat the lamb, or the two will take on one another's personalities; the lamb will become boisterous and the lion will become sheepish-totally out of their character; all because of the one that they chose to constantly associate with.

Note what King Solomon says in Proverbs 27: 17:

17. Iron sharpens iron; so a man sharpens the countenance of his friend.

King Solomon is, in essence, saying that you become like those you that you spend your time with. They become your conosis (Latin word meaning "self pouring". You pour what they are upon you.

You will never feel comfortable enough to grow if you are not associating with someone that completes you, and someone that is most like you.

This principle is the reason why you can put a hundred people in a room; fifty whites and fifty blacks. At the end, when all is settled, you will find that the majority of the blacks will be gathered with the blacks, and the majority of whites will be gathered together with the whites-you are most comfortable with those that are most like you, for allow you the fortitude to "become", or "settle".

If you are to find God's secret place and walk in the light, it is imperative that you journey with others who are seeking God's secret place, or else journey by yourself.

CHAPTER FOURTEEN

GOD'S SECRET PLACE-FILLED WITH GRACE

B efore we journey any further upon the topic of grace, it is of necessity to bring about some distinct clarity to the term "grace". **The meaning of GRACE**: the word grace is pronounced Chen or Chanan in Hebrew, and Charis in Greek (Charis is where we get the word charity from-to give to someone in need that cannot pay you back; this is how it is used in the Holy Scriptures. It literally means "favor"-to bend or stoop in kindness to another- as a superior to an inferior, it has the idea of graciousness in manner or action.

Grace, in the Bible, is usually connected to God's wrath. It is where someone or some people have committed some atrocities (sins) against God's laws, and deserve to be punished and cut off, but **His grace** affords them forgiveness when they don't deserve it, and cannot do anything to earn it, or repay the debt and recover the breach.

Hence, **Grace** is unmerited favor from God; it is divine, unearned, assistance from God. It is a virtue given by God to those that believe in Him.

You cannot earn grace; you cannot buy it; it is only given freely by Jehovah God.

A perfect illustration of grace is Jesus dying on the cross for the sins of human kind. Note what the prophet Isaiah says of Jesus' grace. Isaiah 53: 4-10:

4. Surely he has borne our griefs, and carried our sorrows: yet we did esteem him stricken, smitten of God, and afflicted.
5. But he was wounded for our transgressions. He was bruised for our iniquities: the chastisement of our peace was upon him; and with his stripes we are healed.
6. All we like sheep have gone astray: we have turned everyone to his own way; and the Lord has laid on him the iniquity of us all.
7. He was oppressed, and he was afflicted, yet he opened not his mouth: he is brought as a lamb to the slaughter; And as a sheep before her shearers is dumb. So he opened not his mouth.
8. He was taken from prison and from judgement: and who shall declare his generation? For he was cut off out of the land of the living: for the transgression of my people was he stricken.

9. And he made his grave with the wicked, and with the rich in his death: because he had done no violence, neither was an deceit in his mouth.

10. Yet it pleased the Lord to bruise him: he has put him to grief: when you shall make his soul an offering for sin. He shall see his seed. He shall prolong his days, and the pleasure of the Lord shall prosper in his hand.

What the prophet Isaiah was saying was that Jesus paid a sin debt that he didn't owe for all of mankind who had a sin debt that they couldn't pay.

That is the epitome of GRACE.

Grace, one cannot earn it; one cannot buy or borrow it, and one cannot steal it. It only comes from God-His favor.

His grace is the only way that we can have the ability to live in His secret place and walk in His light.

To find His secret place that is full of grace, and because it is full of grace, it is filled with mercy, we must first acknowledge that we are not worthy of His shelter. His grace makes us worthy.

His secret place filled with grace, gives us gifts that we didn't earn and cannot physically afford.

Grace in His secret place simply puts you in a position where the devil and your enemies cannot touch you, though they want to.

The reason why the Psalmist says that God hides you in His secret place is because He covers up and conceals from the enemy how to get to you.

Grace, simply put, is allowing you access to His secret place and hiding you there where the enemy can't get to you. It is giving you access when you really don't deserve it. And, when you acknowledge the grace of His secret place, it empowers you.

God's grace is His immediate surroundings. If one is in His grace, then one is enclosed in God's presence, which means that he is bathed in Jehovah's power; one is virtually clothed in His Holiness.

The Apostle Paul says that because of His grace, we can enter His presence as though we have never sinned and breached His commandments. Note what Paul says, Hebrews 4: 16:

16. Let us therefore come boldly unto the throne of grace, that we may obtain mercy, and find grace to help in time of need.

The Apostle Paul is saying that because of grace, we can stand before God's throne courageously and boldly as though we have never sinned.

Note how the prophet Isaiah speaks of God towards us- His grace to us. Isaiah 42: 6-8:

6. I the Lord have called you in righteousness, and will hold your hand, and will keep you, and give you for a covenant of the people, for a light of the Gentiles:
7. To open the blind eyes, to bring out the prisoners from the prison, and them that sit in darkness out of the prison house.
8. I am the Lord: that is my name: and my glory will I not give to another, neither my praise to graven images.

Because of His grace, He extends His righteousness to us, thereby, making us righteous. He makes us an example to them that do not know Him; we are the light that show them the way to Him.

His grace gives us access to His glory-the essence of who He is, and His power.

His grace affords us His presence; the opportunity to dwell in His secret place, thereby, abiding with His almighty power and protection against all of the evils of this world, and against the ploys of our enemy the devil.

Remember, grace is God giving us something that we don't deserve, and cannot earned; in this case, the ability to dwell in His secret place and operate under His almighty power.

His grace is Him putting a protective hedge around us so that the devil cannot get to us.

CHAPTER FIFTEEN

THE SECRET PLACE OF
RIGHTEOUSNESS

To live in His **Secret Place**, and walk in His **Light**, we must be righteous. Now, the anchor word in righteous is "right"; so to say that one is righteous, is in essence, to say that one is virtually right-right with Jehovah God.

Thus, righteousness, then, is being good, virtuous, upright, upstanding, decent, moral, ethical, honest, honorable, noble, saintly, and pure.

So hence, we (mankind) cannot live righteous by ourselves, for we have an innate propensity to live unholy lives (sin)-to live contrary to Jehovah's laws.

King David put it this way in reference to being right with Jehovah. He says that one can't ascertain righteousness, in and of themselves, because of who and what we are even from our birth.

Note Psalm 51: 5:

5. Behold, I was shaped in iniquity; and in sin did my mother conceive me.

   David is saying that he (we) was worn born in sin, so therefore, he (we) has an innate propensity to sin. It is in his very being, his very nature, right down to his DNA to live a life of sin.

Observe the Prophet Isaiah's thoughts on the matter of our propensity to live unrighteous lives. Isaiah 53: 6:

6. All we; like sheep have gone astray; we have turned everyone to his own way; and the Lord has laid on him the iniquity of us all.

If we cannot attain a righteous state, the most pervading question then must become "how can we become righteous". The Apostle Paul explains it to us in several passages of scripture. Ephesians 3: 12:

12. In whom we have boldness and access with

Note, too, what Paul says of the matter in Hebrews 4: 14-16/ 5: 1-3:

14. Seeing then that we have a great high priest, that is passed into the heavens, Jesus the Son of God, let us hold fast our profession.
15. For we have not an high priest which cannot be touched with the feeling of our infirmities; but was in all points tempted like as we are, yet without sin.
16. Let us therefore come boldly unto the throne of grace, that

We, obtain mercy, and find grace to help in time of need. 5: 1-3:

1. For every high priest taken from among men is ordained for men in things pertaining to God, that he may offer both gifts and sacrifices for sins:
2. Who can have compassion on the ignorant, and on them that are out of the way; for that he himself also is compassed with infirmity.
3. And by reason hereof he ought, as for the people, so also for himself, to offer for sins.

The Apostle Paul is saying that Jesus is our High Priest (the one that petitions God on our behalf). He goes before God The Father for us and asks the Father to transform our faith into righteousness; thus, **our faith** makes us righteous.

Now, through Jesus our High Priest, we can stand before God in righteousness through our faith. Your faith makes you righteous.

We are as Abraham was; his faith was counted as righteous. Note scripture: Romans 4: 3-8:

3. For what says the scripture? Abraham believed God, and it was counted unto him for righte4ounsness.
4. Now to him that works is the reward not reckoned of grace, but of debt.
5. But to him that works not, but believes on him that justifies the ungodly, his faith is counted for righteousness.
6. Even as David also describes the blessedness of the man, unto whom God imputes righteousness without works,

7. Saying, Blessed are they whose iniquities are forgiven, and whose sins are covered.
8. Blessed is the man to whom the Lord will not impute sin.

Thus, because of our faith, like Abraham, in Him, it makes us righteous; and because we are righteous, we are able to live in His secret place and walk in His light.

WE ARE RIGHTEOUS BECAUSE OF OUR FAITH!!!!!!

Now we are righteous because of our faith in Jehovah's ability to save and keep us from the ploys of the devil. And, because of our faith, we are in His sacred secret place that is full of His light.

CHAPTER SIXTEEN

A TRANSFERRING OF POWER

In His Secret Place

H e that dwells in the secret place of the most high shall abide under the shadow of the Almighty-the 91ˢᵗ Palm.

You don't abide under the shadow of the most high because you just want to hang around Him or just be protected by Him; no, there is much more to dwelling in His secret place and abiding under the shadow of the Almighty.

Something magnificent happens when you are ushered into His secret place; there is a transferring of His omnipotent power upon those that have entered into His place of ultimate holy light; that is the reason why not everybody enters His secret place.

Here is the transferring of power. Note Matthew 11: 27-30:

27. All things are delivered unto me of my Father: and no man knows the Son, but the Father; neither knows any man the Father, save the Son, and he to whomsoever the Son will reveal him.
28. Come unto me, all you that labor and are heavy laden, and I will give you rest.
29. Take my yoke upon you, and learn of me; for I am meek and lowly in heart: and you shall find rest unto your souls.
30. For my yoke is easy, and my burdens are light.

Do you see the transferring of the power that Jehovah gives us that are in His secret place covered by His light.

We are as Jesus. He said that "all things" are delivered into His hands, and so, just as the Father gave him power, so He gives us power. We no longer have to live in fear and defeat any longer; we no longer have to be burdened down by the pressures and stress of life and living; we no longer have to accept defeat. Whatever you are laboring with, you can bring it to Him; no, He commands us to bring it to Him.

He gave us power over all things-real and imagined spiritual and flesh-all things.

I have power over fear, power over my past, power over my failures, power over sickness and disease, power over poverty, and power over all of the power of the enemy and anything and all things that might try to plague me. God delivered to me some of His power to fight against the unholy powers that will fight against me.

He keeps it secret so that our enemy and enemies can't get to us and destroy us.

Notice the distinct power that God gave us. Matthew 10: 1:

1. And when he had called unto him his twelve disciples, he gave them power against unclean spirits, to cast them out, and to heal all manner of sickness and all manner of disease.

That scripture is saying specifically that He gave,too, us power to save and deliver others from whatever shackles that the enemy has placed upon them to bind them up. We have been given the power to fight on their behalf; that means, on behalf of our family, friends, and even some that we don't even know.

When we got into God's secret place, He transferred some of His holy power unto us, and the power of His light illuminates from us. That is how the devil recognizes us as children of God. He sees God's anointed power resting on us. We, as His children, walk in the power that He has transferred to us.

The love that Jehovah has for us is displayed in the book of Jeremiah 29: 11-13:

11. For I know the thoughts that I think towards you, says the Lord, thoughts of peace, and not of evil, to give you an expected end.
12. Then shall you call upon me, and you shall go and pray unto me, and I will hearken unto you.
13. And you shall seek me, and find me, when you shall search for me with all your heart.

Now Jeremiah says this to Israel, Abraham's seed, but it is also referring to all that believe in Christ, for when we believe in Christ Jesus, we become the seed of Abraham. Therefore we are privileged to all of the blessings and power that was bestowed upon Abraham because he is also our father through Christ.

Look at scripture on this matter. Galatians 3: 29:

> 29. And if you be Christ's, then are you Abraham's seed, and heirs according to the promise.

All of these blessings are because of our faith that makes us righteous in Him; and righteousness puts us in "right" relationship with God. The relationship simply means the condition to relate. He relates to us, and we, in turn, relate to Him.

Further benefits of our righteousness in Him are found in the book of Ephesians 6: 10-17:

> 10. Finally, my brothers, be strong in the Lord, and in the power of his might.
> 11. Put on the whole armor of God, that you may be able to stand against the wiles of the devil.
> 12. For we wrestle not against flesh and blood, but against principalities, against powers, against the rulers of the darkness of this world, against spiritual wickedness in high places
> 13. Wherefore take unto you the whole armor of God, that you may be able to withstand in the evil day, and having done all, to stand.
> 14. Stand therefore, having your loins girt about with truth, and having on the breastplate of righteousness:
> 15. And your feet shod with the preparation of the gospel of peace;
> 16. Above all, taking the shield of faith, wherewith you shall be able to quench all the fiery darts of the wicked.
> 17. And take the helmet of salvation, and the sword of the Spirit, which is the word of God.

Paul is talking about all of the power and protection that God the Father gives us because of our righteousness-which comes because of our faith. Remember, we cannot become righteous by ourselves because we have an innate propensity to sin (go against the will of God); and sin banishes you from the presence of God.

Our righteousness gives us access to a power that is greater than any power anywhere.

Observe what the Apostle John says of the power that we possess because of our righteousness. 1 John 4: 4:

4.   You are of God, little children, and have overcome them: because greater is he that is within you, than he that is in the world.

There is a force of power resting in you because of your faith; a power that is greater than any other power outside of God the Father.

Note, he says that you have overcome "them". Who are the "them" that John is referring to- Anybody that shall go against you, or any enemy that you might have.

You will overcome them because God has transferred some of His power unto you, so none can withstand you because you are operating in His power and His might-The shadow of the Almighty.

Look what God says of your power and protection in Isaiah 54: 14-17:

14.   In righteousness shall you be established: you shall be far from oppression; for you shall not fear: and from terror; for it shall not come near you.

15.   Behold, they shall surely gather together, but not by me: whosoever shall gather together against you shall fall for your sake.

16.   Behold, I have created the smith that blows the coals in the fire, and that brings forth an instrument for his work; and I have created the waster to destroy.

17.   No weapon that is formed against you shall prosper; and every tongue that shall rise against you in judgment you shall condemn. This is the heritage of the servants of the Lord, and their righteousness is of me, says the lord.

God is doing all of this because of your righteousness through faith.

Realize the power that God has transferred over to you through your faith- The ability to walk in his shadow and live amongst Him as the angels do.

CHAPTER SEVENTEEN

THE POWER OF LOVE

We have meticulously chosen to conclude this book with love, for love is the epitome of all that we have previously alluded to. It is the quintessential of the faith that makes us righteous and worthy to enter into His secret place under the auspice power of the Almighty.

Observe the importance that Jesus placed upon love in the believer's lives. John 13: 34-35:

> 34. A new commandment I give unto you, That you love one another; as I have loved you, that you also love one another.
> 35. By this shall all men know that you are my disciples, if you have love one to another.

Jesus stresses to His disciples the importance of love. He says to us that this is a new commandment; you must love each other. Note, He says that that is how men (of the world) will know that you are my disciples-you will love one another. In essence, Jesus followers will sacrifice for each other; feed each other; fight for each other, and even deny themselves for each other-they will have unfeigned love for one another.

Everything that I have fore stated hinges on love; love makes everything work, and holds everything together. You will never enter into Jehovah's secret place without love, and you will never experience the power of The Almighty without love.

Well, let us take an in-depth look at love.

Love, in its literal sense, is a human emotion-which often times rule the other emotions that we have, or at the very least, it deeply influences the other emotions.

It is the most misunderstood emotion that we possess. It has been written about; talked about, studied, and some have even made movies on the emotion of love.

And, everybody wants to feel the euphoric anastasia of love. It is a feeling that evokes all kinds of feeling and other emotions are enhanced because of love. It has made strong me weak, and weak men strong. Love has made wise men foolish, and foolish men wise.

Love is most elusive, but all men and women chase it, and passionately want to feel the fangs of love planted deep within their hearts.

Let us first observe the literal meaning of love.

Although many will define love as one with many definitions, however, there are essentially only four definitive kinds of love-the rest are built upon or from these. The four kinds of love are:

1. Eros
2. Philia
3. Storge
4. Agape

Let analyze them separately:

Eros-It is that kind of love that is filled with passion and desire. It is the stimulator or end result of the other kinds of love, and the one that makes the possessor excited, tremble, and become overly elated while filled with joy. Eros makes one's breaths short and quick, and the blood pressure elevate. Eros is highly expressed between a husband and wife (legally expressed with Jehovah's blessings). Eros love deals deeply with feelings of the body between two individuals. The end result is usually consummation between the two lovers. Eros was the love between Solomon and the queen of Sheba, or the love between Samson and Delilah

Philia, is that deep love between friends and comrades. It is geared towards one's natural taste and preferences. Philia is the feeling that you feel between people that you have chosen that are most like you-people that you trust and believe. Philia is the love that was in the bible between the friends David and Jonathan.

Storge, is the collective love one has for their community and family. It is a natural carnal love usually built upon blood relationships. Storge is a love that is primarily built upon previous relationships-community, family.

Agape, is that godly sacrificial kind of love; a love that is filled with grace and forgiveness. It looks beyond one's faults and sees one's needs. It is the love that God has for human kind, His creation. Agape love is the reason why Jehovah sacrificed his son, Jesus Christ, for us. Agape is that love that is unwavering, all forgiving, and all caring. It loves in-spite of, not because of. Agape is the love that Jesus was instructing His disciple to have for one another. I love you regardless of your weaknesses, failures, and shortcomings. I love you with a God kind of love; that is Agape love. Agape is that kind of love that the prophet Hosea had for his unfaithful wife Gomer, and Samson had for Delilah.

The Apostle Paul speaks of agape love when he penned his epistle to the church of Corinth. Observe 1 Corinthians 13: 1-8 / 13:

1. Though I speak with the tongues of men and of angels, and have not love, I am become as sounding brass or as tinkling cymbal.
2. And though I have the gift of prophecy, and understand all mysteries, and all knowledge; and though I have all faith, so that I could remove mountains, and have not love, I am nothing.
3. And though I bestow all my goods to feed the poor, and though I give my body to be burned, and have not love, it profits me nothing.
4. Love suffers long, and is kind; love envies not; love vaunts not itself, is not puffed up.
5. Does not behave itself unseemly, seeks not her own, is not easily provoked, thinks no evil;
6. Rejoices not in iniquity, but rejoice in the truth;
7. Bears all things, believes all things, hopes all things, endures all things.
8. Love never fails: but whether there be prophecy, they shall fail; whether there be tongues, they shall cease; whether there be knowledge, it shall vanish away.

13. And now abides faith, hope, and love, these three, but the greatest of these is love.

Paul is asserting that love is the greatest thing that you can have and the greatest thing that you can desire. It is both a weapon and a shield of protection.

One cannot operate in His secret place and possess His almighty power is you don't walk in agape love.

Note the power that Jesus says that you will acquire when you are in Him. John 15: 7:

7. If you abide in me, and my words abide in you, you shall ask what you will, and it shall be done unto you.

Look at the power that we have when we dwell in His secret place. Jesus said that you can ask whatever you want, and it shall come to pass.

Now you understand why love is so important; because if you are not operating in love, then you will destroy more people than you will help.

Even while living for Him, and abiding in Him, agape love is so important because you will still have some battle to fight, and some struggles to go through.

You have got to love, and love, and love, and love, and love.

And, when you walk in agape love, you have found His secret place, and have access to His almighty power.

CHAPTER EIGHTEEN

YOUR NEXT STAGE OF LIFE

H ere-to-fore, we have only discussed the comfort of have security in this life through God, but we would be remiss if we did not, at the very least, some exegesis upon our journey to the next life-the hereafter.

Many times, we get so caught up in this life, until we forget that there is another life, another stage of life.

We must not put all of our hope in this life, of what we can accomplish and come to possess, for there is life after this life.

The reality is we shall soon go down a road of which no travelers return.

And, this is inevitable, so we must prepare now for our next journey into the next life.

Note what the Apostle Paul says of the matter; Hebrews 9: 27:

27. And as it has been appointed unto men once to die, but after this the judgment.

This is an appointment that you cannot break, and it does not matter who you are, or what you have. You have got an appointment wit death.

I observe the world around us amidst all of its chaos; of racism, riots, turmoil, and distress, and I wonder to myself, do they not realize that they shall exit this life soon. I say soon because it does not matter how long one lives, in comparison to time eternal, we only live a moment.

Observe what Job says of man's life; Job 14: 1-2:

1. Man that is born of a woman is of few days, and full of trouble.
2. He comes forth life a flower, and is cut down: he flees also as a shadow, and continues not.

Job says that man does not live long, and that his life is filled with troubles.

Man searches for fulfillment in things and stuff, and many sometimes hope that they can validate their lives by seeing others as villains; thereby, justifying their unjustified corrupt actions.

It matters not how rich or poor you are; it matters not your position upon earth, whether you are a president, a king, a dictator, or pauper, all must soon exit this life and enter into the next; whether you are Donald Trump, Kim Jong-un, or Vladimir Putin, you shall soon leave this life and enter the next.

Because we shall soon die, we must ready ourselves right now, and how do we do that?

The bible says that how you prepare yourself for the next life is through accepting Jesus Christ as your savior. Romans 10: 9-13:

9. That if you shall confess with your mouth the Lord Jesus, and shall believe in your heart that God has raised him from the dead, you shall be saved.
10. For with the heart man believes unto righteousness; and with the mouth confession is made unto salvation.
11. For the scripture says, Whosoever believes on him shall not be ashamed
12. For there is no difference between the Jew and the Greek: for the same Lord over all is rich unto all that call upon him.
13. For whosoever shall call upon the name of the Lord shall be saved.

We must be ready to exit this life; that is why we must walk in love, because how ever we exit here, is what we shall meet in the hereafter-we shall reap what we have sown in this life.

Observe 2 Corinthians 5: 1-4:

1. For we know that if our earthly house of this body were dissolved, we have a building of God, a house not made with hands eternal in the heavens.
2. For in this we groan, earnestly desiring to be clothed upon with our house which is from heaven.
3. If so be that being clothed we shall not be found naked.
4. For we that are in this body do groan, being burdened: not for that we would be unclothed, but clothed upon, that mortality might be swallowed up of life.

In essence, what Paul is saying is that, in this life, we must live life in such a way that it prepares us for the life to come.

Observe what the bible says of us facing, in the next life, what we have done in this life. Galatians 5: 7-8:

7. Be not deceived; God is not mocked: for whatsoever a man sows, that shall he also reap.
8. For he that sows to his flesh shall of the flesh reap corruption; but he that sows to the Spirit shall of the Spirit reap life everlasting.

So worry not yourself of haters, racist, supremist, klu Klux klansmen, racial bigots of any color, or any one that fosters hate and injustice, for they shall surely come face to face, in the next life, with their own demons.

I've watched unjust policemen beat senseless innocent citizens; I have seen on the news where rioters clash with one another and leaving some bloodied and bruised, and some even dead; and I think to myself, do they not realize that they are going to stand, in their next life, before the judging, all mighty God; He does not care whether you are black or white, or Indian.

God judges us upon the merit of the life that we have lived in this life. So, hence, the life that you are living now is preparing for the kind of life you shall live after this present life.

You see, it is not a matter of whether you are going to live eternally, for you shall; the prevailing question is where will you live forever?

Because God created you and breathe His breath in you, you cannot be completely destroyed. Your body can be destroyed, but the real you, the inside you can never die.

Note what Jesus says of the matter. Matthew 10: 28:

28. And fear not them which kill the body, but are not able to kill the soul: but rather fear him which is able to destroy both soul and body in hell.

Isn't that simply amazing; a short time on earth will determine where you will spend eternity.

Don't you think that if Adolf Hitler could come back, before he killed millions upon millions of Jews, he would choose differently?

Your actions in this life will determine the condition of your life in the hereafter.

Again, listen to Jesus: John 11: 25-26:

25. I am the resurrection, and the life: he that believes in me, though he were dead, yet shall he live:
26. And whosoever lives and believes in me shall never die

Jesus is saying that, in fact, this life is not the end of the story; He is saying that he has the power to raise you up again after death.

The longest part of your living is the next life; your present life is but a fleeting moment.

Observe what James says of the matter on life: James 4: 13-14:

13. Go to now, you that say, Today or tomorrow we will go into such a city, and continue therea year, and bu and sell, and get gain:
14. Whereas you know not hat shall be on tomorrow. For what is your life? It is even a vapor. That appears for a little time. and then vanishes away.

TALK RIGHT

A man's belly shall be satisfied with the fruit of his mouth; and with the increase of his lips shall he be filled.

Death and life are in the power of the tongue: and they that love it shall eat the fruit thereof.

Proverbs 18: 20-21

BELIEVE RIGHT

Believe in the lord your God, so shall you be established; believe his prophets, so shall you prosper.

2 Chronicles 20: 20

THINK RIGHT

And be renewed in the spirit of your mind;

And that you put on the new man, which after God is created in righteousness and true holiness.

Ephesians 4: 23-24

WALK RIGHT

For we walk by faith and not by sight.

2 Corinthians 5: 7

YOUR LIFE IS FILLED WITH WHAT YOU TRULY BELIEVE

Therefore I say unto you, what things so ever you desire, when you pray, believe that you receive them, and you shall have them.

Mark 11: 24

Change what you have been accepting and believing, and believe God's blessing for you, and watch your life change, and your conditions **turn around**!!

CLOSING PRAYER FOR YOU

Now unto him that is able to keep you from falling, and to present you faultless before the presence of his glory with exceeding joy,

To the only wise God our Savior, be glory and majesty, dominion and power, both now and ever, Amen.

Jude 1: 24-25

NOTES

NOTES

NOTES

NOTES

NOTES

NOTES

NOTES

NOTES

NOTES

NOTES

Printed in the United States
By Bookmasters